OSPREY COMBAT AIRCRAFT • 40

PBJ MITCHELL UNITS OF THE OF THE PACIFIC WAR

SERIES EDITOR: TONY HOLMES

OSPREY COMBAT AIRCRAFT • 40

PBJ MITCHELL UNITS OF THE PACIFIC WAR

Jerry Scutts

OSPREY

PUBLISHING

Front cover
Searchlights are an irritation to any combat crews obliged to operate at night, and this held true for the Marines who flew the North American PBJ Mitchell in the Pacific in World War 2. Leading a flight of PBJ-1Ds on a 'heckling' mission to the Japanese-held town of Kavieng, on New Ireland, on the night of 26 November 1944, the aircraft flown by Lt Col George A Sarles was caught in the cross beams of no fewer than four searchlights.

Then commanding officer of Marine Corps squadron VMB-611, Sarles decided to do something about this source of annoyance. He promptly winged over and dived straight down one of the beams. At 1500 ft he salvoed a pair of underwing high velocity rockets into the blinding white light. Enemy flak gunners probed in vain for the plunging PBJ, and the rockets found their mark. Sarles' crews were suitably impressed at this feat on the part of an officer held in high regard by everyone in the squadron.

VMB-611 later transferred from the South-West Pacific Area to help wrest control of the Philppines from the Japanese. George A Sarles continued to lead his Marine aircrews on numerous hazardous low-level strikes until he was killed in action on 30 May 1945. All who survived the war having served in combat with VMB-611 said that the unit never fully recovered from his tragic loss (*cover artwork by Mark Postlethwaite*)

For a catalogue of all Osprey Publishing titles please contact us at:

Osprey Direct UK, PO Box 140, Wellingborough, Northants NN8 2FA, UK
E-mail: **info@ospreydirect.co.uk**

Osprey Direct USA, c/o MBI Publishing, 729 Prospect Ave, PO Box 1, Osceola, WI 54020, USA
E-mail: **info@ospreydirectusa.com**

First published in Great Britain in 2003 by Osprey Publishing
Elms Court, Chapel Way, Botley, Oxford, OX2 9LP

ISBN 1 84176 581 3

Edited by Tony Holmes and Bruce Hales-Dutton
Page design by Tony Truscott
Cover Artwork by Mark Postlethwaite
Aircraft Profiles by Jim Laurier and Scale Drawings by Mark Styling
Index by Alan Thatcher
Origination by Grasmere Digital Imaging, Leeds, UK
Printed by Stamford Press PTE, Singapore

03 04 05 06 07   10 9 8 7 6 5 4 3 2 1

EDITOR'S NOTE
To make this best-selling series as authoritative as possible, the Editor would be interested in hearing from any individual who may have relevant photographs, documentation or first-hand experiences relating to the world's elite pilots, and their aircraft, of the various theatres of war. Any material used will be credited to its original source. Please write to Tony Holmes via e-mail at: tony.holmes@osprey-jets.freeserve.co.uk

ACKNOWLEDGEMENTS
The author expresses his thanks to the US Marine Corps Historical Division, the US National Archives and the Smithsonian Institution, all of whom supplied numerous photographs, copies of war diaries and background data. In addition he is pleased to thank Alan C Carey, Robert F Dorr, Jack Lambert, George Let, the late Robert Millington and the Royal New Zealand Air Force Historical Division for supplying photographs. North American Aviation, through the good offices of Gene Boswell and Norm Avery, also contributed photographs illustrating many aspects of the development and testing of Marine Mitchells for combat. Special thanks are due to Thomas D Honeycutt for providing *Cram's Rams,* his history of VMB-612, and Raymond S Berry, who kindly loaned a copy of *The Bombers of MAGSZAM,* his fine published history of VBM-611.

CONTENTS

'FLYING NIGHTMARES'

The Unites States Marine Corps' contribution to victory in World War 2 is remembered principally for the bloody land campaigns to eject the Japanese from their island garrisons on the 'road back' from Pearl Harbor. The need for air support to protect friendly ground troops and attack the enemy became clear during the early part of the conflict, although Marine Corps commanders had recognised the need for their own organic airpower during the 1930s.

Single-engined fighters and dive-bombers were acquired via Navy contracts, and they proved invaluable in preventing the Japanese from taking control of the Solomon Islands in one of the earliest land battles of the Pacific war. But such aircraft had one major drawback – they were very short-ranged, and therefore obliged to wait for the enemy to come to them rather than mount offensive operations to relieve the pressure on the ground troops by attacking the enemy in rear areas.

The need for aircraft with a longer reach had to be addressed and, anticipating the day when multi-engined bombers would be available specifically to support its ground forces, the Corps approached the Navy to procure suitable aircraft. There were two reasons for the Navy's reluctance to allow the Marines to operate bombers – budgetary concerns and the belief that naval squadrons could provide the necessary air support. Actual combat proved this thinking only partially valid, for if enemy forces were committed to a lengthy campaign, a high number of bomber sorties was required to dislodge them, and enable territory to be captured.

As the struggle to wrest control of the Solomons from the Japanese developed, part of the hastily assembled 'Cactus Air Force' defending the strategically important island of Guadalcanal was Marine Air Group 23, a mixed fighter and bomber formation. On 21 August 1942 it was announced that the F4F Wildcats of VMF-223 had assumed the honour of being the first aircraft to offer direct air support 'by Marines for Marines' during the Battle of Ilu River. Repelling the enemy's assault on the Marine perimeter, the Wildcat pilots forged an enduring link between their own air power and ground forces – one that endures to the present day.

The idea of Marine squadrons operating aircraft larger than Wildcats and Dauntlesses had been put forward in 1941 by Brig Gen Ross E Rowell. The following year, with the country now at war and enormous changes in US airpower taking place, it was agreed that B-25 Mitchells would be supplied via Navy procurement channels.

It was clear that if the capture of Japanese island outposts was to mean further amphibious landings by the Marines, Army and Navy air forces might be hard pressed to provide adequate air cover in a protracted land

Apart from its Navy patrol bomber blue and white finish, the PBJ-1C as delivered to the Marines in 1943 was little different to a standard Army B-25C, complete with retractable ventral gun turret. USMC modification centres soon altered the bomber's appearance, particularly when radar was installed

PBJ-1D BuNo 35094 *JONAH* shows how far the ventral radome for the scanner could be lowered, although in service this was apparently fixed in the less extended position seen in the photograph at the top of page 12. The wing bomb racks introduced on the C-model can just be discerned (*North American Aviation*)

campaign. Carrier strikes and pre-invasion bombing might not be sufficient. Furthermore, following the US government's agreement to a 'Europe first' war policy, the Pacific theatre could not immediately be supplied with great numbers of aircraft. Range was always a major consideration for the USAAF when operating in the Pacific. Its heavy bombers were usually able to reach outlying islands, but their generally small-scale missions were of necessity interspersed with periods when the enemy enjoyed a respite. On the other hand, if Marine medium bombers, dive-bombers and fighters could be based closer to the action, troop casualty levels could at least be contained by continuous, smaller scale bombing missions aimed at keeping the enemy constantly engaged.

Having developed a doctrine of providing their own air support wherever possible, Marine Corps commanders eagerly accepted the Navy's offer of B-25 Mitchells. As the furthest ranging patrol bombers in-theatre, they were to be based as near to the frontline as possible, thus allowing them to offer assistance, frequently at short notice.

It is often said that the B-25 did not have a specific role when it was offered to the Navy in substantial numbers, and this was true enough. The service already operated the medium-range Lockheed PV Ventura (see *Osprey Combat Aircraft 34 - PV Ventura/Harpoon Units of World War 2* for further details) and the long-range PB4Y-1. The Marines' need for longer-range aircraft meant that virtually the entire Navy allocation of the North American medium bomber would be transferred to it. That represented a force of some 700 aircraft at a time when the Corps was

building its independence in the crucible of war. Fortunately, the B-25 was to prove one of the most versatile aircraft used anywhere in World War 2, and a suitable role could therefore be found for it when the bomber entered service with the Marines.

Designating the Mitchell as the PBJ-1 (P for patrol, B for bombing and J for North American Aviation), the Corps took delivery of its first examples in February 1943, and then set about deciding how best it could be deployed. These early Mitchells were designated PBJ-1C and 1D, the equivalents of the Army's B-25C and D respectively. The designations denoted similar aircraft built at North American's Inglewood and Dallas plants, but extensive modifications would ensure that any direct comparison with Army machines was at best incidental.

It was decided that most Marine mediums would have radar like that developed for Army B-25s previously engaged on anti-submarine and 'sea search' missions off the US coast. The AN/APS-3 set was therefore installed in the PBJ-1C's belly in place of the ventral turret. The aircraft proved invaluable for training crews in radar operability prior to operational deployment. It emerged from official deliberations that the Marine Corps' mission of 'heckling' – attacks on targets from forward airfields by radar-equipped medium bombers, preferably at night – would suit the PBJ. Such operations as an adjunct to those conducted during daylight hours would deny the enemy any respite, and wear down his ability to resist. Anti-shipping strikes by PBJs were also envisaged to deny the Japanese vital sea borne supplies for island garrisons.

UNIQUE TRAINING

With the delivery of the first 50 PBJ-1Cs to add to a small inventory of Beech SNB trainers – themselves among the Corps' first 'twins' – the

The 'H' aerial under the cockpit of VMB-612's PBJ-1D 'Mike Baker 37' enabled the aircraft to be picked up by GCA (Ground-Controlled Approach) radar to aid landing in bad weather and at night. Extra ammunition boxes for the front guns may be seen through the nose windows, above the horizontal rod aerial (*via Thomas Honeycutt*)

The most obvious change to the PBJ was the installation of a radar scanner in the nose of the aircraft as an alternative to mounting the equipment ventrally. Dubbed the 'hose nose' or the 'schnozzle' (after Jimmy Durante), this arrangement was preferred by many bombardier-navigators as it reduced the level of 'sea clutter' on their scopes to a bare minimum (*Smithsonian*)

The pilot's view over the 'hose nose' radome was not as restricted as might be assumed. Several instruments were also moved within the cockpit following the fitment of the nose radome, the repeater compass, for example, taking the place of the rev counters on the instrument shroud (compare with the photograph on page 11). The crossbar to the extreme right of the photograph was associated with the torpedo release sight (*Smithsonian*)

Marines established an intensive training programme. Personnel volunteering for transfer to a Marine bomber squadron would encounter several unique procedures. Anticipating that forward area servicing might be adversely affected by lack of groundcrews, loss of equipment and scant facilities, each six-man PBJ crew was trained not only to fly their aircraft in combat, but to service it as well. Radar operator training was given high priority. Although the USAAF had gained some experience with B-25s so equipped, the programme had not been expanded after the Navy took over the sea search mission. It therefore fell to the Navy, via the Marines, to develop its own operational techniques for effectively deploying radar-equipped mediums in an offensive role.

Quite early in the PBJ training programme, the AN/APS-3 search radar was given a redesigned scanner housing which allowed it to be fitted into the nose of the PBJ and sweep straight ahead. This radome, faired above the bombardier's position, was quickly dubbed the 'hose nose'. It was the distinguishing feature of many PBJs, and was preferred by aircrews as its 145-degree forward scan provided a less cluttered picture on the scope than had been the case with the original belly-mounted scanner – the latter suffered serious interference from the sea. Later model PBJ-1Js had the radome mounted on the right wingtip. This gave much the same

This PBJ-1D carries a prominant training base code on its nose. Aircraft with both a 'K' and an 'R' prefix were flown from Cherry Point, Boca Chica and Edenton, all in North Carolina, which was the home state for the PBJ training organisation. This view shows to advantage the humped housing over the tail gunner's position, developed as a modification by North American Aviation for the early Mitchells which lacked tail defence. Marine aircraft had a single tail gun (*via Alan Carey*)

coverage, but it was common for squadron technicians to relocate the scanner in the nose for convenience. That said, the 360-degree sweep of the belly-mounted scanner was most effective (sea clutter aside), especially when flying at night over islands in a storm.

Providing the Marine mediums with reliable search data, the APS-3 radar had a useful range capability either vertically downwards with a belly mounting or as a horizontal scan with a 'straight ahead' nose or wing mounting (*North American Aviation*)

The clear images appearing on the pilot's five-inch scope – adjustable to five-, 20- and 100-mile ranges – stood out so well that each landmark could be compared with a map. Some pilots claimed that using the ventral radar was as good as flying visually. Combat operations did not require every PBJ to be fitted with radar, and in the closing stages of the war late model PBJ-1Hs and Js flew in 'factory configuration' with their wing-tip radomes in place. Whether or not a PBJ carried radar depended on the operating unit, and the type of missions being flown.

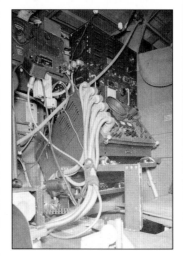

Inside the PBJ the degree of plumbing needed for the radar and the scope was considerable, making the navigator-bombardier's compartment quite cramped. The Marines still managed to cram the aircraft full of guns, however (*Smithsonian*)

Establishing a training programme from scratch with few personnel or aircraft, and only a vaguely-defined operational goal, took patience and perseverance. At first, Marine aviation cadets reporting to the main PBJ training base at Cherry Point, North Carolina, spent most of their time at ground school until enough instructors were available to initiate flying training. Any new programme suffers its share of teething troubles, and this was no exception. There was scant background for an organisation with hundreds of men under intensive training for an entirely new concept. With aircraft deliveries increasing, and a rising number of trainee crews reporting for duty, the

This PBJ-1D boasts a more or less standard dual control cockpit layout, complete with two RPM indicators on the panel coaming. Directly below them is a 'caged' torpedo release handle, which may have temporarily displaced the rev counters on this particular aircraft. The large artificial horizon and compass give a clue to the aircraft's medium and low altitude attack role (*Smithsonian*)

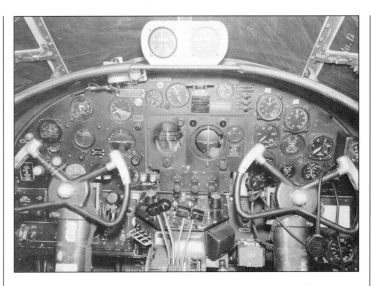

A flashback to 1943, and training days at Edenton, North Carolina. This VMB-413 PBJ-1D is marked with small forward fuselage numbers similar in both size and style to those employed by the squadron in combat. Ambitious, but not totally realised, plans for the PBJ programme meant that training continued almost until the end of the war (*J V Crow*)

Marines established Operational Training Squadron 8 (OTS-8). Among the first personnel transferred to OTS-8, and the PBJ programme, were reservists who were relieved of their current (ground) duties and ordered to report to Cherry Point. Ten first lieutenants, subject to a transfer order dated 9 July 1943, were destined to become the original flight officers of the initial PBJ unit, VMB-413.

'TRADITIONAL WEAPON'

It was natural enough, given the historic precedents, that Marine officers charged with training medium bomber crews would place an emphasis on the aerial torpedo as a PBJ attack weapon. Consequently, carriage and launch equipment was provided for the PBJ-1C to deploy a single 22-in Mk 13 aerial torpedo on an external rack below the fuselage. North American and Marine Corps engineers worked out the technical adjustments necessary to tailor the B-25C to its new role, including the development of a reliable torpedo sighting system for use by the pilot and co-pilot. A considerable amount of work went into perfecting the sighting system, and tests were flown with several aircraft, including *JONAH*, the workhorse PBJ-1D (BuNo 35094). Trainee combat crews

also carried out numerous dummy torpedo runs which showed that the PBJ was quite capable had attacks on shipping been part of its assigned duty. But somewhere along the way, and certainly before any PBJ went into action, the requirement for Marine medium bombers to undertake torpedo attacks was shelved.

By mid-1943 it was considered that the air-launched torpedo had passed its heyday. Bombs had proven highly effective against shipping, Army B-25 units in particular having pioneered a range of operational techniques, including skip-bombing, to deal effectively with maritime targets. But this did not entirely remove torpedo attack from the PBJ's repertoire, and wartime training continued to include torpedo release techniques. The Army did not entirely rule out the use of such a weapon either, as B-25s later deployed a new type of glide torpedo in the Pacific.

This left the PBJ-1D – which introduced under-wing bomb racks – as a more or less conventional medium bomber with an internal bomb-bay capable of carrying up to four 500-lb or 20 100-lb bombs or depth charges, plus up to 1000 lbs of ordnance on four under-wing racks. Having proved reliable with US and Allied B-25 units, the gravity bomb would remain the PBJ's primary offensive weapon. Indeed, the Corps had every intention to deploy medium bombers in such a role, stating in 1943 that 'the primary mission of bombing squadrons is high, horizontal air attack, and it is highly probable that these squadrons will be used on search attack or bombing missions in which there is an additional (mission) of reconnaissance'.

While acknowledging the Army's low altitude horizontal skip-bombing tactics and the Navy's own torpedo attacks, the report recognised that for the Marine bombers to emulate such feats modifications to bomb racks would be required. In the event the standard production version of North American's versatile medium fitted Marine Corps requirements, being roomy enough to accommodate new electronic equipment and capable of carrying a

JONAH and other early PBJ-1Ds that were passed to the Marines were heavily modified as shown here, and apart from the torpedo, this aircraft was typical of the first PBJ-1s to see combat. The national insignia has the 1943 red outline over-painted with insignia blue (*Smithsonian*)

A busy scene at Peter Point Field, with PBJ-1Ds of VMB-612 pulled close into a hangar so the crew can take advantage of the small amount of shade afforded by the roof overhang. Modifying the PBJs for combat was a round-the-clock job for the Marine groundcrews, some of whom arrived with scant experience of fitting the essential radar and radio sets. All aircraft destined for overseas duty had to be modified accordingly

range of ordnance for low to medium altitude attack on sea and land targets. Few Marine trainees regretted the end of torpedo attacks. Always demanding and often hazardous in the face of enemy opposition, the 'low and slow' approach required for launching a torpedo was an additional hazard that PBJ crews would no longer have to face.

Army B-25s had also brought the deadly art of strafing to a new peak in early Pacific operations. The Marines took due note, and while it was deemed prudent – at least initially – to retain nose glazing rather than to cover it all up and fill the bombardier's space with additional machine guns as some Army units had done, heavy gun armament was also to mark the early model PBJs. A typical PBJ-1D configuration was three 0.50-cal machine guns in the clear nose, four side-mounted in the fuselage and two in the mid-fuselage dorsal turret. The number of guns was boosted to 12 with hand-held weapons operated from rear fuselage side hatches.

By removing the transparent tail cone, a single 'fifty' was installed to protect the PBJ from stern attack. In this respect Marine Mitchells differed from the Army's B-25Cs and Ds, which retained the tail cone fairing. Depot and field modifications added a tail gun position with a humped fairing, which the PBJ-1D also used. Some PBJ-1Cs and Ds also featured two further guns mounted to fire from the corners of the convex 'bay windows' designed for the B-25H and J. Set forward just aft of the wing trailing edge, these positions made for a rather crowded centre section, but the additional Plexiglas areas proved useful for observation as well as defence.

Although the eight-gun 'strafer' nose designed to fit all B-25 models could not offer the Marines quite the same mission versatility as the standard glazed fairing, some PBJs nevertheless boasted the former. It is believed that the actual total of strafer PBJs was quite small, most if not all being conversions using field kits. The 75 mm cannon fitted to G- and H-model B-25s was retained by the PBJ-1H, although it proved somewhat difficult to tailor the 'big gun' Mitchell to Marine Corps operations. As the Army had discovered, bombs and rockets, in particular, could deal with virtually any target with less risk to the attacking aircraft than using guns. As with torpedoes, an accurate cannon attack required a steady,

As the first PBJ units entered combat operations in the South Pacific, the following ones continued to hone their skills. Various bases were used for specialised weapons training, among them Paxutent River, the Navy's major test facility in Maryland. This PBJ-1D (35176/MB-200) is pictured on the flightline at Pax River on 1 March 1944 (*via Robert F Dorr*)

straight and level approach. In addition, neither of the 'solid nose' B-25 configurations could accommodate radar.

FIRST SQUADRON

Aware that their radar-equipped aircraft still gave them a considerable edge over conventional medium bombers in anti-shipping attacks, Marine cadets undertook eight weeks of intensive training. Those who followed would generally perpetuate the techniques that had originally been established. As the first Marine Corps PBJ medium bomber unit, VMB-413 was commanded by Maj Robert B Cox and subordinated to Marine Air Wing 3. The squadron was commissioned on 1 March 1943. A month previously, Marine Air Group (MAG) 61 was organised at

Marine medium bomber crews put in hundreds of training hours mainly because aircraft in the PBJ class had not been operated before, and radar bombing and night 'heckling' were roles with few precedents. These five 'hose nose' PBJ-1Ds were assigned to VMB-612, and the variable treatment of the radome tips is notable, as this area was supposed to be coated with a vegetable-oil based paint to avoid corrosion (*via Thomas Honeycutt*)

Espiritu Santo, in the New Hebrides, was a waypoint for Marine squadrons heading for their forward combat areas. It grew into a major supply base for all US air forces fighting in the South Pacific. This evocative photo shows PBJ-1Ds dispersed among the coconut palms in 1944 (*IWM*)

Cherry Point, its function being the administration and maintenance of eight squadrons of PBJs. Having moved to Espiritu Santo by mid-1944, MAG-61 sailed for Emirau on 12 July, where it remained until the war ended. All 'first echelon' PBJ units based in the South-West Pacific Area were attached to MAG-61.

IMPROVED COMMAND

US military direction of the Pacific war was changed considerably in the light of experience from the Solomons campaign, during which numerous hard lessons were learned. By the summer of 1943 ComAirSols (Commander, Air Forces Solomons) comprised US Army, Navy and Royal New Zealand Air Force (RNZAF) multi-engined bombers, dive-bombers and fighters, with the Marines contributing dive-bombers and fighters but initially no medium bombers. By the time the first PBJ squadron was ready to move overseas, the war in the South Pacific had stabilised from the Allied viewpoint.

ComAirSols' autumn 1943 offensive against the Japanese on Bougainville, combined with Fifth Air Force attacks on Rabaul, had enabled the 3rd Marine Division to land at Cape Torokina, opposite Buin, on New Britain. The division encountered 23,000 troops commanded by Gen Hyakutake, most of whom were located on the other side of a central mountain range. The presence of this force brought about a protracted campaign which saw Marine SBDs flying close support missions as the Japanese attempted to 'go round the mountain' to relieve the 2000 defenders at Torokina and destroy the Marine bridgehead. This proved impossible, and further Allied pounding of Rabaul, which lasted into February 1944, brought about the stunning loss of more than 300 Japanese aircraft and forced a mass withdrawal from the New Britain bastion to Truk, in the central Pacific. This left Rabaul all but devoid of air cover, although some Imperial Japanese Navy cadres remained.

At the same time Kavieng, in New Ireland, part of the Solomons chain, was also largely abandoned by the Japanese, although a nucleus of defensive personnel was to give Marine PBJs a few headaches, not least by manning searchlight and flak batteries. The fire from these guns, although described in reports as 'meagre', hardly looked that way to crews unused to being shot at.

These withdrawal moves by the Japanese effectively (and unexpectedly) opened the 'road to the Philippines', and brought about changes in US strategy. Recent battles had left the Imperial Navy chronically short of experienced pilots as well as aircraft. But garrisons remained on both islands, and while they could be bypassed, they still had to be contained. Left undisturbed, there was every risk that the Japanese would attempt to reinforce Rabaul and Kavieng and use their airfields to attack Allied supply lines. Astute deployment of US aircraft in the most important forward areas could neutralise any likely threat in line with the policy of imposing an aerial blockade. That was where the PBJs of VMB-413 came in.

NEW COMMANDER

On 30 June 1943 Maj Cox was replaced as the CO of VMB-413 by Lt Col Ronald D Salmon. He would lead the squadron until its combat debut under Lt Col Andrew B Galatian Jr. But there was still some

15

question as to where the Marine mediums would be most effective, and consequently the eagerly-anticipated move overseas was not to take place until early December, when the squadron's 15 PBJs flew to North Island Naval Air Station. It was to be 3 January 1944 before the bombers were loaded aboard the carrier USS *Kalinin Bay*, bound for Hawaii and Marine Air Station Ewa, west of Pearl Harbor. A weak hook on a Ford Island crane caused VMB-413's first PBJ loss during unloading at Pearl Harbor, and a second aircraft was lost en route between Canton and Samoa when three aircraft flew into a tropical front and only two emerged.

VMB-413 was the first PBJ squadron to see combat. Beginning operations on 15 March 1944, the squadron 'wrote the book' on night 'heckling' by attacking Rabaul, Kavieng and other bypassed garrisons, interspersing night sorties with numerous daylight missions. Local conditions in the South-West Pacific soon took their toll on the pristine finish of these PBJ-1Ds, photographed on 28 March 1944 (*USMC via Robert F Dorr*)

Understandably, the Marine Corps wanted photographic evidence that medium bombers could carry out a new mission well, and a series of stills was taken during VMB-413's debut mission on 15 March. On this date four tons of bombs were dropped on installations between Rapopo and Tobera airfields, ten miles south-east of Rabaul. A flight of four PBJ-1Ds is seen here (*USMC*)

The PBJs neared the combat zone when they arrived at Espirito Santo, in the New Hebrides. Finally, in March 1944, VMB-413 was installed at Stirling Island, in the Treasuries group. The two losses meant that squadron strength was now down to 13 aircraft even before operations had started, and combat and general attrition would inevitably whittle this down still further. The squadron had originally planned to fly 12-ship missions, holding three aircraft in reserve at all times. This ratio, however, had demonstrably allowed little margin for loss.

RABAUL OFFENSIVE

The Marine crews were assigned to fly missions to Rabaul, a place that would become synonymous with their early operations. Dominating Simpson Harbour – one of the finest natural anchorages in the South Pacific – the town had been occupied by the Japanese since January 1942, but from 12 October 1943 attacks by the US Fifth Air Force had effectively blockaded the port and harbour. When the depleted air units of the Japanese Navy departed in late 1943, most of their personnel had also been withdrawn. Consequently, by the time the Marine mediums got into

action, that area of New Britain was relatively quiet. But Rabaul still had teeth. Driven into underground bunkers, the Japanese established supply dumps and maintained communications with the outside world.

Anti-aircraft defences continued to claim victims, and the Allied high command responsible for the region felt it could not afford to ignore Rabaul completely. A primary reason for this wariness was the five airfields that encircled the town – Lakuani, Vunakanau, Rapopo, Keravat and Tobera. Although they were kept under surveillance, and regularly bombed, the beleaguered Japanese set about rebuilding several of the wrecked Mitsubishi A6M Zeros left behind when the bulk of their forces were evacuated to Truk. Undetected by US reconnaissance flights, they achieved this feat of engineering by utilising 15 A6M airframes at Lakuani. One Mitsubishi Ki-46 'Dinah' reconnaissance type and various other out-of-commission aircraft, including four Nakajima J1N1 'Gekko' nightfighters, also remained.

NIGHT 'HECKLING'

By the time VMB-413 was ready for operations against Rabaul, US, Australian and New Zealand airpower had greatly reduced the garrison's effectiveness. Most air operations were conducted in daylight, and it was decided that to contain Rabaul on a 24-hour basis, Marine PBJs would carry out 'heckling' missions mainly at night. Initially, in order to familiarise crews with the terrain of New Britain, daylight sorties were flown with the PBJs bombing in formations of up to nine aircraft at a time, carrying HE bombs ranging in size from 100- to 500-lb. The first such mission for VMB-413 was undertaken on 14 March 1944, the target being a supply dump situated at Takubar Mission, ten miles north of Rabaul. The attack resulted in 82 out of the 84 bombs released by the formation falling squarely on the target – a 'job well done' signal was sent to the unit from ComAirSols.

The squadron flew eight sorties on the 15th to hit a labour camp and barracks at Vunapope. Again the bombing was accurate, with 82 out of 96 500-lb GP bombs falling in the target area. Strikes on 16 and 17 March produced equally good results considering the small size of the targets and the relative inexperience of squadron bombardiers. As VMB-413 began hauling bombs to Rabaul on a regular basis from its first combat base on Stirling Island, Emirau, in the St Matthias Group, was being secured and prepared to operate aircraft. Daytime sorties for the unit continued, with further runs to Takubar and Vunapope. Daylight PBJ sorties were shared with USAAF and RNZAF bombers and fighters, the latter being available for escort when necessary.

When Emirau was secured as a US base, the Marine PBJs

As an introduction to combat operations in the South-West Pacific, Marine PBJ squadrons flew many standard medium altitude formation bombing missions and dropped a range of bombs, the smallest being 100 'pounders' and the largest 2000 'pounders' (*USMC*)

were located above New Britain. Working with those based on Stirling Island, at the lower end of Bougainville, the bombers could, by staging through Green Island (several hundred miles nearer to New Britain), conveniently sandwich the main enemy strongholds at Rabaul and Kavieng between two points of the compass. Combat

A PBJ-1D of VMB-413 approaches Simpson Harbour during the week of 15-20 March 1944. This aircraft was flying over St George's Channel when the Marine photographer in an accompanying Mitchell took this shot (*Robert Millington Collection*)

flights could therefore avoid over-flying too much hostile territory, the trade-off being marginally less hazardous ocean crossings to and from the targets. These sorties familiarised the American crews with the combat area and operational conditions prior to VMB-413 concentrating on regular night 'heckling' missions.

From late March the pattern was usually a nine-ship daylight mission flown every third day, interspersed with anti-submarine sorties to add variety. But at night the PBJs had the sky virtually to themselves, forcing the long suffering defenders of Rabaul and Bougainville to endure further deprivations. VMB-413 sent out two or three aircraft on nights when conditions over the target areas were forecast to be clear enough for bombing.

Missions were planned and executed with great care, as all personnel were made aware that the entire PBJ programme rested on the results achieved by VMB-413. That being so, no air organisation based in the Pacific, however smoothly run, could overcome the negative effects of the weather. This was to prove more hostile to Marine PBJs than the Japanese. Indeed, when the exact circumstances of a crew failing to return could not be determined, the weather became the prime suspect.

Adopting a system of designating one aircraft as section leader, VMB-413 initially followed Army practice. But whereas Army flight crews were always officers, the Marines adopted the Navy system of putting both commissioned and non-commissioned personnel in the cockpits of its medium bombers. This caused some problems, as few badges of rank were worn in the combat area. That this system was sound was frequently

A mixed formation of PBJ-1Ds of VMB-413 head for their target, with 'hose nose' aircraft in evidence in the lower flight below Mitchell '411', which almost certainly had its radar housed in a ventral radome. Not all PBJs were equipped with radar, however (*USMC via Alan Carey*)

proved when individual NCOs demonstrated superior operational skills, particularly in navigation and bomb aiming accuracy. One such individual was T/Sgt Joe Deceuster, navigator/bombardier in Robert 'Oak' Millington's crew. Millington, who usually flew PBJ-1D BuNo 35126, rated Deceuster the squadron's best navigator-bombardier, an accolade that was well deserved.

As VMB-413 honed its collective night vision over Rabaul, targets were hit hard – but at a price. A particularly bad night was 22/23 March 1944 when A6M Zeros intercepted and shot down the PBJ flown by Maj James K Smith before it had reached its objective. There were no survivors from the six-man crew. Being intercepted by Zeros over Rabaul came as something of a shock to the crews. It was rumoured that a small number of fighters were still based there, but this was one of the few occasions when an American aircraft was actually lost to one. The bombing of Rabaul's five airfields was stepped up, as was the laying waste of any building that might house the defenders' precious fighter repair facilities.

When night 'heckling' became VMB-413's primary mission, the unit adopted the nickname the 'Flying Nightmares'. It was appropriate, and it stuck. Instead of the more garish unit badges adopted by other PBJ squadrons, VMB-413 went for a low-key lucky green shamrock, but with the number 13 defiantly painted across it. Vern Aiken was a member of a PBJ crew during this period, serving as a tail gunner with Capt Andy Berstrom's crew. Aiken liked to add a little explosive spice of his own in the form of 20-lb anti-personnel bombs. As the PBJ released its main load of 14 100-lb GP bombs, the gunner would open the bottom hatch and, straddling it, drop the small bombs out one at a time, pulling the pin securing the arming vanes on each before it fell away.

Flying night 'heckling' missions no matter what the weather meant a taxing time for VMB-413's crews. Having battled their way through torrential rain, strong winds and pitch darkness, their first point of reference might be Japanese searchlights and hostile flak, with the additional threat of nightfighters to keep them alert. On 16/17 April Bob Millington almost became the victim of a J1N1 'Gekko', two of which were based on Rabaul. As the PBJ commenced its bombing run, the enemy fighter opened fire. American gunners tried sighting on the Japanese aircraft but it sheered off before they could draw a bead, and it was not seen again.

ABSORBING LOSSES

Combat attrition was beginning to hurt VMB-413 as spring 1944 brought further sorties and more losses. Nevertheless, the squadron's groundcrews wrought their usual miracles and no aircraft were lost to mechanical failure. On 5/6 May Col Galatian led six PBJs to Tobera to destroy a large supply dump. Approaching the target at 12,000 ft, the Mitchells were greeted by heavy flak through which the formation

On 3 May 1944 VMB-413's PBJ-1Ds took another crack at a Japanese island target, their radar assisting the 'bombing through overcast' method also adopted by the USAAF (*USMC via Robert F Dorr*)

ploughed on to release 71 100-lb bombs. Reaching the release point, the PBJ of 1Lt Glen Smith took a direct hit in its port engine. Despite his bombardier salvoing the bomb load, the Mitchell spun down in flames. There were no survivors.

Summarising his time with VMB-413, Bob Millington considered the PBJ to be a stable, dependable aircraft which could fly well on one engine, provided the propeller on the dead powerplant could be feathered. The PBJ did not respond well to flying with a wind-milling prop. 'My only objection to the PBJ was lack of speed', Millington recalled. 'We were loaded down with ten 0.50-cal

machine guns, and later two more "fifties" with ammunition. We had a 265-gallon bomb-bay fuel tank and wing racks for eight 100-lb bombs, and with the A/S "George" radar (APS-3) antennae hanging from the belly, speed was considerably reduced'. In an emergency, PBJ crews could contact several bases by VHF radio to report emergencies – provided they were in range;

'We could contact Stirling Island, which was codenamed Terrier Base, and Bougainville (Dane base), but the radio was not good for more than 50-75 miles. Later, we were able to contact Munda, Green Island and Emirau on VHF if we were close enough. We had an emergency radio in the rear of the aeroplane, operated by key, and to use it we dropped a long, trailing antenna on a leaded weight. The purpose of this radio was to reach Bougainville for reports. The call number was "Zero-Zero-Baker-One", but we were seldom able to raise them. No contact was made, for example, on that night in April when I was jumped by an "Irving" and we could not warn the aeroplanes coming after us that nightfighters were about. We sometimes made contact with PT boats, but in general our emergency system was miserable.'

As Millington previously mentioned, the PBJ was not the fastest thing in South Pacific skies, particularly when fully loaded with fuel and ordnance;

'I can remember climbing to reach 10,000 to 12,000 ft, fully loaded with 110-gal of gas, at an indicated airspeed of 132 knots before reaching targets in the Rabaul area. Our standard cruise speed never exceeded 160 knots indicated, and on low-level missions, even by diving to get more speed, we seldom exceeded 200 knots.

'The highest speed I ever obtained in a PBJ was on a special low-level mission which saw the aircraft carrying only 600 gallons of gas and four 500-lb bombs. I squeezed 219 knots IAS (Indicated Air Speed) out of the bomber, which, on that occasion, boasted just one nose gun – the turret weapons and all the aircraft's fuselage-mounted machine guns and ammunition had been removed. Personally, I wished we could have had the British Mosquito.'

Flying over another South Pacific island holding far less menace than New Britain, a PBJ-1D circles Stirling Island, home base for the first operational PBJ squadrons. VMB-413 flew many missions from Stirling during its inaugural combat tour (*Robert Millington Collection*)

This PBJ in dire straits was flown by 1Lt Glenn Smith of VMB-413. Hit in the port engine by heavy flak 10,000 ft over Tobera airstrip on 5 May 1944, the aircraft later crashed with the loss of the entire crew. Although combat casualties among PBJ squadrons were quite light considering the number of sorties flown, crew losses were deeply felt (*Robert Millington Collection*)

'SEA HORSES' AND 'DEVILS'

On 15 May 1944 the 'Flying Nightmares' were relieved by the second frontline PBJ unit, Lt Col John L Winston's VMB-423 This squadron would hold the line for two months until VMB-413 returned in July. ComAirSols was fulsome in its praise for what the original PBJ unit had achieved in carrying out the new and highly-demanding mission of night 'heckling'. Indeed, the Marine flyers had found a role that could not be filled by any other current aircraft type.

Like its predecessor, the newly-arrived unit flew the PBJ-1C/D and maintained the night 'heckling' of the Japanese from Stirling Island. Placed under the temporary command of MAG-14, pending the arrival of MAG-61, VMB-423 began operations on 17 May 1944. Its first mission was a nine-aeroplane, medium-altitude day attack on Namatanai, New Ireland. The first night sorties came shortly afterwards, when crews spent over six hours 'heckling' Rabaul. Once again, bypassed Japanese bases in New Britain represented the main land targets for the newly arrived PBJ squadron.

The welcome view many PBJ crews saw on return from a mission – the approach to the Stirling Island strip. The island's location put the Marines' principal targets well within range of their PBJs (*Robert Millington Collection*)

Submarine patrols also continued for the time being, one VMB-423 crew spending ten hours orbiting in the Bougainville area with nothing to report at the end of it. That these search missions were rarely fruitful was illustrated by another crew which spent five hours on a vain search in the teeth of raging thunderstorms, only to have their aircraft burst a tyre on landing back at base and be totally written off in the ensuing crash. Fortunately no crew casualties were suffered to add injury to insult.

On 25 May a VMB-423 crew went to war on behalf of the schoolchildren of Oklahoma. As part of a US public war bond drive to buy new aircraft, 35,000 youngsters had collected money and signed their names on a 65-ft scroll, and Gen Mitchell thought it would be a nice touch to present it to the enemy on the next PBJ raid. He sought crewmen from Oklahoma to fly the scroll to Rabaul, but only SSgt Bill Woolman and Lt Dick Morgan qualified on that count. There was nothing for it but to swear in the other four crewmen as honorary Oklahomans for the sortie, which duly set out to leave its 'calling cards' (explosive and paper) on Rabaul's Rapopo airfield.

Although it was not over-publicised, Japanese flak was a fact of life for PBJ crews attacking the bypassed islands of the South Pacific. Sometimes it could be deadly enough to bring down the Marine bombers, although to an untrained observer the weight of fire was described as 'meagre' (*USMC*)

Escorted by F4Us, Morgan's PBJ reached the target, and while bombs were dropping on the runway the scroll was released from a waist hatch. Attached to a parachute and weighted down by a machine gun barrel, the paper streamer should have drifted right into the enemy-occupied area, but it somehow apparently failed to do so. The Japanese therefore failed to learn the extent to which America's children were supporting their fighting men.

Moving base on 21 June, VMB-423 then operated from Nissan, the largest of the offshore atolls forming the group known collectively as Green Island. While 'heckling' raids to Rabaul tended to slacken off during the long summer days and short nights, the number of medium altitude strikes increased. Various targets from Kavieng to the southern tip of New Ireland and all across the Gazelle Peninsula were hit by VMB-423's PBJs. As the squadron had been the first in the Corps to perfect skip-bombing and strafing, several shipping targets were also attacked, but with unknown results.

During the summer the Marine unit witnessed what turned out to be the 'last gasp' effort by Rabaul-based fighters to intercept its aircraft. On 9 June two A6Ms attacked Lt William J Hopper's PBJ during a 'heckling' mission to Vunakanau airfield. Hopper said later;

'Our squadron mission at that time was to be over the Rabaul area from 1800 to 0600 hrs, surveying the area with radar during the night so as to be aware of any ship or aeroplane movement, and to harass by dropping bombs on any lights we might see.'

Having dropped a 100-lb bomb on Tobera airfield, Hopper flew to Vunakanau at 10,000 ft, only to be spotted by Japanese fighters. His crew had no way of knowing that one of the enemy pilots, CPO Fumio Wako, had already destroyed a VMB-413 PBJ. In March Wako's victim had been the aircraft flown by Maj Smith, but adding a second PBJ to his score proved impossible

PBJs often made their approach to Rabaul over St George's Channel, although the direction would often be dictated by the weather. These VMB-413 aircraft were participating in an early 1944 squadron mission (*Robert Millington Collection*)

on this occasion. Flying as wingman to flight leader CPO Yasushi Shimbo, Wako made four runs on the PBJ in section right echelon, the wingman positioned some 20 yards behind his leader. Hopper's evasive flying ensured that no shells struck his aircraft, and in a dogfight that ended inconclusively, none of the PBJ's gunners hit the Zeros. The Marine crew continued with its sortie, dropping three more 100 'pounders' on Vunakanau and their last on Lakunai, before returning to Green Island at 2125 hrs.

This interception came as quite a surprise because only a handful of Japanese aircraft were believed to remain on New Britain's airfields after the mass withdrawal to Truk. The Imperial Japanese Navy's Air Group 253 scraped together a handful of A6Ms and the few pilots and groundcrew managed (despite the parent unit officially being disbanded on 10 July 1944) to maintain a presence at Rabaul until the end of hostilities. There were few further contacts with PBJs. All participants in the inconclusive air battle of 9 June had the good fortune to survive the war, Hopper himself going on to fly 100 missions with VMB-423, and win the DFC.

Despite the survival of Hopper's crew, the ill luck that had apparently attached itself to VMB-423 from the earliest days – the squadron had lost five PBJs before entering combat – struck again on the night of 22 June. 1Lt Vernon R Kistner and his crew of seven took off from Green Island and were never heard from again. The casualties included intelligence officer 2Lt Thornwell Rogers. A PBY picked up a flight jacket 48 hours after the PBJ went missing, indicating that the aircraft had gone into the sea, probably off Duke of York Island. A further loss came one week later June when Capt Richard A Edmond's crew was lost when their aircraft crashed on return from a 'heckling' mission. This disaster could not be blamed on the weather, however, for the PBJ was making a normal approach with the runway lights on when it hit trees. The left wingtip was torn off, starting a chain reaction which ended with the aircraft going off the end of the runway and into the sea.

In July it was decided that VMB-423 would not be relieved in its entirety, but would instead remain operational, with five crews at a time taking recreational leave in Australia. On the 19th Lt Col Norman J Anderson took over the squadron, which simultaneously had its nickname 'Sea Horse Marines' approved, along with an insignia depicting an armed, fire-breathing seahorse against a white cloud rent by lightning flashes. The promotion of Anderson was a good augury, for he went on to fly a total of 107 missions.

THE 'DEVILS' ARRIVE

Green Island became a little more crowded on 16 July with the arrival of nine PBJs belonging to Lt Col Gordon 'Art' Adams' VMB-433, the third Marine Mitchell squadron to see combat. More aircraft duly flew in during the course of the following weeks, and by August the unit had reached its full complement of 15 aircraft. After VMB-433 had settled in, PBJ pilot Malcolm L McGuckin designed a squadron insignia comprising a fork-tailed dragon astride an aerial torpedo carrying a bomb and firing a machine gun. A dog named 'Whiskey' became squadron mascot at around this time, and he subsequently accumulated 404 hours of flight time before being run over and killed on Emirau in 1945. Not to be outdone in the nickname stakes, VMB-433 chose to call itself the 'Fork-Tailed Devils'.

Making its combat debut on, or about, 13 August 1944, VMB-433 struck Vunapope, the 12-ship mission being led by Lt Col Adams. By that time the unit had 26 flight crews available for operations, although its own ground echelon remained for a time on Espiritu Santo. Consequently, aircraft maintenance was carried out by VMB-423 crews.

It appears to have been Marine Corps policy to train each PBJ unit to demonstrate a speciality within a broadly similar curriculum. For VMB-433 it was formation flying at night, its crews claiming that they could get 12 Mitchells into the air and join up in echelon – a demanding feat that they had extensively practised. Skip bombing and strafing had also been daily fare for the Marine flyers. The ability to acquire such skills also spoke volumes for the thorough training all PBJ units underwent before assignment to a combat zone.

In addition to broadening the PBJ's combat capabilities as far as possible, the Marines ensured that experienced personnel passed on their wisdom in the most practical way. For example, VMB-433's executive officer was Maj Robert Cox, VMB-413's first CO. After its operational debut, VMB-433 moved to Emirau in late August. New crews of the freshman squadron flew with both VMB-413 and -423 in order to gain experience before becoming an integral part of MAG-61 on Emirau.

On 13 July an advance echelon of VMB-443 (the fourth and last of the original quartet of PBJ squadrons) arrived on Emirau under the command of Lt Col Dwight M Guilotte. It began combat operations immediately after the flight echelon's arrival on 13 August. Operational sorties, again in PBJ-1C/Ds, followed the pattern set by the other PBJ squadrons, VMB-443's crews also having gained combat experience by flying in VMB-413 aircraft for several shakedown missions.

With more aircraft on hand, MAG-61 could put up quite large formations of PBJs (up to 30 aircraft) for its continuing war against the bypassed enemy bases. Ordnance loads were also boosted, the PBJs

A VMB-433 PBJ-1D clears the trees after take-off and climbs out at the start of yet another nocturnal mission. VMB-433 flew tedious bombing and 'heckling' missions to Rabaul for almost a year, despite its senior officers continually asking MAG-61 for better targets (*via Alan Carey*)

A PBJ usually carried a crew of six. Posing for the camera are, back row, from left to right, Bill Parks (pilot), Chick Higbie (co-pilot) and Weyman Carter (navigator-bombardier), and front row, from left to right, Percy Deputy (tail gunner), Don Synold (turret gunner) and Henry Leonard (radioman)

occasionally carrying a single 2000-lb GP bomb in the fuselage bay. Such a weapon was intended finally to break up the concrete runway at Vunakunau. Tobera, and the other three airfields at Rabaul, also received this heavyweight Marine 'calling card'.

Forming up such large formations of PBJs from different units resulted in several collisions. On 27 February 1945 12 aircraft each from VMB-413 and -433 joined up for a mission to Rabaul. As they did so, a VMB-433 aircraft collided with one from VMB-413, the latter piloted by Maj Cunningham. This was seen to fly off on a north-westerly course and disappear, and there are indications that Cunningham was the sole survivor of the ensuing crash. The VMB-433 PBJ, piloted by Donald R Harpley, fared little better. Badly damaged by the impact, it fell out of formation and ditched off Emirau. Only co-pilot Archie R McAllister was rescued.

SECOND TOUR FOR VMB-413

When VMB-413 returned to combat operations, its new PBJ-1C/Ds were based at Munda, New Georgia. The squadron, which continued to be led by Lt Col Galatian, operated independently of its three sister PBJ units from July through to October 1944, before also becoming part of MAG-61. When VMB-413 did return to the fray, it was not long before Bob Millington was shot down.

Japanese gunners arranged a hot reception for the five-ship flight sent to attack a supply dump at Choiseul on 29 July, and Millington's PBJ was hit in the starboard engine. A wing tank ominously started leaking fuel, and tail gunner Tommy Thomas suffered a flesh wound. As the crippled aircraft crabbed out over New Georgia Sound, it was clear it would not fly much further – certainly not as far as Barakoma, an airstrip on Vella Lavella, as the skipper was hoping. The PBJ ditched and all the crew left in a hurry. Two hours later they were picked up by a PBY.

The upshot of this indignity was that 'Oak' Millington was offered an opportunity to get his revenge by making a solo attack on a 430-ft Japanese freighter, the *Kihili Maru*, beached off southern Bougainville. Defended by the embarked guns and flak batteries located on nearby Kangu Hill, the enemy had continued to use the ship as an offshore headquarters for several high-ranking officers. It was a prime target. Millington freely admitted he

En route to Rabaul from Stirling Island, this VMB-413 PBJ-1D has the simple white aeroplane-in-squadron identification numbers used by the first Marine medium bomber squadron to see action (*Robert Millington Collection*)

Tediously familiar to PBJ crews who saw it repeatedly throughout 1944 - 45, the Japanese stronghold of Rabaul, on New Britain, may well have given the Allies a headache had it been left alone. It was the job of the Marine bombers not to leave it undisturbed. This view, taken from the north by a VMB-413 PBJ flying at about 11,000 ft, clearly shows Simpson Harbour

was quite 'gung ho' in those days and, despite dire warnings from other crews that the strike was a suicide mission, jumped at the chance to destroy the freighter. Having stripped the PBJ back to its bare essentials, the crew took off on their low-level sortie on 9 August.

Racing across southern Bougainville with Kangu Hill to starboard, the PBJ climbed suddenly then dropped back down. Millington bored straight in with his gunners firing fit to burn out their barrels. Four 500-lb bombs were on their way in an instant, plunging straight for the ship's side. When they hit, the *Kihili Maru* crumpled up, its centre section wreathed in flames. It was in dire straits as the PBJ pulled away. Once back at base, the crew were recommended by Maj Gen R J 'Pete' Mitchell USMC, Commander of Aircraft, Northern Solomons, for an official commendation. He added in a telegram, 'Give the "Peter Baker Jig" crew that socked the *Kihili Maru* a well done from Mitchell'.

Missions from Munda were familiar enough to any crew members who had already done one tour with VMB-413 – night 'heckling' of eastern areas of Bougainville, medium altitude bombing and strafing of enemy targets on the Shortland Islands and low-level strafing and bombing of Choiseul. The major difference now was that Rabaul no longer figured

While some of their comrades were finding out what combat was like, other Marine flyers were discovering that training was not always smooth and easy. This 'hose nose' PBJ-1D suffered a comparatively rare main gear leg collapse and other repairable damage following a heavy landing (*via Robert F Dorr*)

A pair of 'Flying Nightmares' PBJ-1s drop 100-lb bombs on Keravat airfield, near Atkikilkum Bay. This was one of five airfields surrounding the New Britain stronghold of Rabaul which were continually pounded to prevent their use by Japanese fighters and bombers (*Robert Millington Collection*)

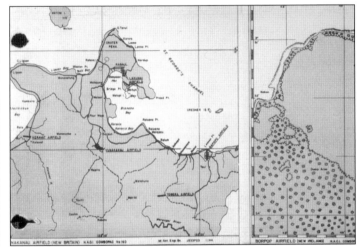

The Rabaul area became so familiar to PBJ crews that they could almost find it blindfolded. Maps, such as these, were nevertheless issued! (*Robert Millington Collection*)

regularly in the unit's target list, this particular hot spot being left in the increasingly-experienced hands of VMB-423, -433 and -443.

As before, VMB-413 embarked on its second tour with several daylight sorties, Lt Col Andrew B Galatian Jr leading the first mission of his own second tour on 29 July 1944. The targets were ports and inland positions on Sipasai and Guppy, the PBJs receiving a hot reception after repeat runs to destroy a Japanese defensive position in Tarekekori Village.

EMIRAU

When MAG-61 moved to Emirau the PBJ squadrons continued with medium altitude bombing in small formations – pretty routine sorties that not everyone exactly warmed to. Harvey Schiener was one of VMB-413's pilots who indulged in a little low-level work to break the monotony.

Having been briefed for a night 'heckling' mission, Schiener dropped part of his bomb load then dived for a close look at the New Britain coast. Sweeping along the shoreline, the PBJ reached Rabaul just before sunrise. Going downtown with some bravado, the PBJ swept along the main street, firing its nose and turret guns, before banking off towards a land spit on the eastern side of the island. Here, the PBJ dropped its remaining bombs, and the crew had the satisfaction of seeing a large explosion which they guessed was an ammunition dump.

Such low level attacks appeared to yield positive results, and on 8 September 1944, VMB-433's Capt Gene Bable went on a dawn sweep of the New Ireland coast. When the PBJ passed over Kavieng at 10,000 ft, there was no noticeable enemy activity, then a crewman reported seeing a wake a mile or two offshore – Japanese barge traffic was known to operate in the area and Bable dropped to 500 feet. He lined up on the barge and opened fire. After two more runs the wake disappeared and the PBJ crew, assuming the vessel had been sunk, resumed their patrol.

Once back at base the awful truth about the target was made known – the Marine crew had attacked an American PT boat. Bable was exonerated, principally on the grounds that the intelligence officer has specifically stated at the briefing that no friendly vessels were likely to be in his patrol area. But the Emirau Island commander, believing that pilots and crews clearly failed to appreciate Navy surface operations, directed that the Marine airmen were to go on a PT mission. It was an experience few of them forgot. More importantly, there were no further incidents of PBJs firing on PT boats. As was demonstrated later in the Philippines, co-operation between Marine bombers and PT boats was generally very good.

On 4 August further moves towards the seemingly inevitable invasion of Japan were made when the four MAG-61 PBJ squadrons were ordered to move from Bougainville to the southern Philippines. That this order was not complied with immediately is demonstrated by the fact that all four squadrons were still on Bougainville by the 9th – the day they carried out the final Marine medium bomber attack on Rabaul.

It had been a long, tedious and dangerous haul for aviators and defenders alike, but from the US viewpoint the job had been done. Apart from several inconclusive offensive sorties by Rabaul's tiny air force, the base had been neutralised.

VMB-433 armourers inspect the breeches of the port twin 0.50-cal package guns fitted to a squadron PBJ-1D. Operated by the pilot, the four 'cheek' guns gave a useful spread of fire during strafing runs. Good maintenance access was provided via a single downward-hinged panel (*Henry Sory via Alan Carey*)

PBJ-1Ds 'Black 301' (left) and '302' wait to receive their loads from trailers hauling bombs and armourers out to the flightline. Neither the squadron nor the location are confirmed, but VMB-413 on Stirling Island almost certainly fit the bill (*via Alan Carey*)

NEW WEAPONS

Having acquired examples of all B-25 combat models, the Marines, like other US services, found those aircraft fitted with a 'bombardier nose' to be best suited to their operational needs. Alternatively, all B-25 models could be quickly adapted for the strafer role by substituting the short 'solid nose' containing either a 75 mm cannon and two or four 0.50-cal machine guns, or the 'long nose' mounting no fewer than eight 'fifties'. The Marines acquired examples with both configurations, although it was commonly agreed by the US services that the heavy

cannon was only effective if the target merited attack with such a weapon. It is obvious that any field modification to create a PBJ strafer had to substitute a bombardier nose for a solid one, since it was hardly very practical to do it the other way round. Most Marine Mitchells retained the tried and tested PBJ-1D configuration with a bombardier, as night 'heckling' had not envisaged much strafing. That would change when the PBJ arrived in the Philippines, however.

Having tested the PBJ-1H's armament over Pacific firing ranges, Marine crews had been duly impressed with the 75 mm cannon, which promised to be a capable weapon. It was therefore decided to issue the H-model to VMB-614 – the last PBJ squadron to be based in a combat zone. There was, however, little opportunity for much action because enemy shipping had by then become scarce. The problem now facing the unit, as Army B-25H squadrons had previously discovered, was finding targets that warranted 75 mm cannon ammunition and, having done so, making the necessary straight and steady approach into the teeth of the defences. Stuck on an ocean atoll, VMB-614 really wanted some worthwhile shipping because there were few alternative 'big gun' targets within PBJ-1H range.

PBJ-1D 'Black 27' was flown by the VMB-413 CO, Andrew Galatian, seen here lined up with his crew – back row, from left to right, 2Lt George Knauf, Lt Col Galatian and 2Lt Robert Cox, and front row, left to right, Sgt Leo Gervis, S/Sgt Paul McCastland and Sgt Mike Viparina

Integrating the PBJ-1H into existing operations proved as difficult for the Marines as it had for the Army. This was because of a lack of suitable targets, particularly shipping, requiring the attention of the 'big gun' Mitchell. Down in the grass at Cherry Point on 14 July 1944, PBJ-1H BuNo 89017 was on the strength of VMB-614, the seventh and last Marine Mitchell outfit to prepare for combat. Actually, the nearest it got to any Pacific action was Midway Island in 1945 (*Dave Lucabaugh via Robert F Dorr*)

29

Having commissioned the first four '400 series' PBJ squadrons, the Marines then designated four more as '600 series', and although eight others were subsequently formed, the operational units would all be drawn from these two original groups. VMB-611, -612, -613 and -614 were all commissioned at Cherry Point on 1 October 1943.

ROUGH PASSAGE

With training completed, orders were cut for VMB-611 (the first squadron of the second series) to prepare to sail for the Pacific – it turned out to be very unfortunate that half of the unit's flight crews and all the ground echelon boarded the freighter *Zoella Lykes* at Port Hueneme, north-west of Los Angeles. It would take these men five months of tramping around the Pacific at the whim of a disgruntled skipper before they were reunited with the squadron's main flight echelon. After some delay as a result of changing the invasion points in the Philippines, VMB-611 left Hawaii on 22 October 1944 and had island-hopped its way to Emirau by 27 October. The PBJs flew Palmyra Island-Canton Island-Funafuti-Ellice Islands-Espiritu Santo-Munda-Emirau. There were mishaps en route, and only 11 aircraft arrived, but Col George A Sarles immediately organised a maintenance schedule.

It was in these circumstances, with groundcrews still sweating out their enforced ocean cruise, that the PBJ units' training paid off. With each member of the five-man crews able to handle a secondary speciality – the turret gunners were ordnance-men, waist gunners were radio-men and so forth – the PBJs were checked over thoroughly and a spares inventory drawn up. Everything the squadron needed was available at the supply depot on Finschafen, in New Guinea, so the colonel led ten PBJs on a 'shopping trip'.

A few shakedown sorties were duly flown to Kavieng, and on the night of 16/17 November 1944 Sarles marked his unit's combat debut with a run on a nearby airfield, accompanied by Maj Dick Maulsby as his wingman. Both PBJs were armed with five-inch rockets, which had a range of 2.5 miles, plus or minus 100 yards, at elevations of 4000 to 6000 ft. These figures were the basis for determining the location of firing points along a

Two airfields on the northwest tip of Emirau Island became the last base for the PBJ squadrons of MAG-61. North Cape and Inshore airfields were simple, one runway and facilities, with the ocean at each end. This PBJ is flying in from the sea over well laid out access roads adjacent to one of the airfields (*via Alan Carey*)

The four wing racks fitted to the PBJ-1D accepted a variety of ordnance including depth charges, which were occasionally used against land targets. Here, armourers load standard 250-lb GP bombs (*North American Aviation*)

Allies – Marine PBJs regularly joined units of the RNZAF in strikes on Rabaul and other enemy locations. Here, a pair of PV-1 Venturas of No 1 Sqn fly in formation with a PBJ-1J in December 1944. The PBJ lacks radar and, unlike its Lockheed contemporaries, carries no external ordnance (*RNZAF*)

predetermined flight line towards the target area. Range was calculated from an easily-recognised land mass far enough beyond the target so that release on such a firing point would cause the rocket to fall on the target. The action report of this initial mission described what happened;

'The aeroplanes went to a point five miles due north of North Cape, Kavieng and orbited. As one PBJ would make a run, the other remained at 10,000 ft to act as cover. As soon as the rockets were fired, evasive action was taken in the form of a bank away from the direction of fire. Five searchlights were employed unceasingly against the "hecklers", and meagre to light flak was seen, as well as a few heavy bursts above the PBJs.'

The Japanese managed to cone the PBJs in their searchlights before the rockets were fired, and although everyone soon realised that the anti-aircraft fire was light, and would have seemed inconsequential in daylight, it was heart-stopping at night. The enemy may not have had a vast number of guns on Kavieng, but he was usually able to concentrate fire on a few aircraft. Crews just had to get used to it, although some never did. There was a general consensus that guard duty in the Solomons was not the picnic described by some who had never flown over the hot targets.

On 22 November Sarles and three other VMB-611 crews returned to Kavieng, where they dropped depth charges and fragmentation clusters, as well as rockets. The bombs were aimed by the Mk 15 Norden sight from 9500 ft after the rocket runs, and an attempt was made to vary target approach both in angle and altitude. All ordnance reportedly hit the target squarely. Three days later four PBJs dropped 500 million candlepower photoflash bombs over Kavieng to blind the searchlight crews, and the American airmen noted a marked delay in both the lights coming on and the flak starting.

The following night (26th) a series of strikes by a succession of two-ship sections witnessed a dramatic gesture on the part of Sarles. Four lights were probing the sky for the PBJs, and VMB-611's CO promptly winged over and attacked one. Flying down one of the beams, with flakshells bursting all around his aircraft, Sarles let fly with two rockets at 1500 ft and the light suddenly went out. Crews who saw their CO's daring act were duly impressed.

The rest of November was occupied by further runs to Kavieng, some including photographic sorties as well as a radar searches for reported enemy aircraft, which was called off. Routine training flights were also undertaken. Then, on 11 December, the target was Rabaul. That morning Sarles led nine PBJs (armed with a total of 27 100-lb bombs) on the two-hour flight to New Britain, the PBJs heading for Lukunai airfield .

On the way the Marine bombers were joined by an RNZAF Ventura

31

1Lt Herb Lentsch poses in the cockpit of his PBJ-1D after his 26th mission with VMB-413. As the original PBJ squadron, the 'Flying Nightmares' accrued more operational missions than the others for the remarkably low loss of just 33 men and seven aircraft (*Herb Lentsch*)

squadron, as well as an escort of Marine F4U Corsairs. Coming in from the sea, the crews spotted the airfield, situated below Rabaul town. Crouched in the nose of Sarles' aircraft, M/Sgt John McGee adjusted his sight as the Japanese flak gunners found the range. Correcting for drift and involuntary banking due to shell bursts, McGee opened the bomb-bay doors and released. Sarles banked the PBJ away to the left as the rest of the formation went through a similar procedure, aiming to spread the bombs along the length of the runway.

In mid-December VMB-611 finally located its groundcrews on the *Zoella Lykes* at Ulithi. But despite recriminations, the captain, who had no orders to unload his ship, only released 13 of the flight crews! The groundcrews would have to sit it out for many more weeks before the old freighter made its way to the Philippines. There, the right paperwork would finally persuade the skipper that he could legitimately unload his human cargo. This was a time of confusion for the squadron, as orders were received that VMB-611 was to head for Luzon in January 1945. The location and date was then changed to Mindanao in March.

In any event, it was good to have the missing aircrew – who had not flown since July – assigned to active duty. Lt 'Moe' LeMasters was one of the first pilots to sample war over Kavieng in late December. Climbing to 10,000 ft, his PBJ headed for the target area on automatic pilot. It was 70 miles to Kavieng. Suddenly, the aircraft ran into a thunderhead. Almost immediately the ASI dropped to 90 mph, then back up to 300 mph as the PBJ plummeted towards the sea. Rain lashed the bomber, water finding its way between the plates and soaking the pilots to their knees. Then the PBJ was through the storm, but by then LeMasters felt enough was enough. Weather fronts were lethal, and he ordered the bombs dropped in the ocean before heading back to Emirau. It was a wise precaution.

On 17 January Lt Charles H Lawrence and his crew got lost on a training flight. The night was so dark that truck lights had to be used to guide the aircraft in, but they could barely be seen from the air. Lawrence came in first but misjudged his angle of approach. Before he could clear the trees, the PBJ plunged into the jungle, bursting into flame. The entire crew, rated as one of VMB-611's best, died in the crash.

In February 1945 the unit enjoyed an interesting period of training after the squadron had received orders to join Col Jerome's MAGSZAM (Marine Air Group Zamboanga) on Mindanao. There, the missions would often be at low level, so Sarles instigated a series of 'zero feet' sweeps over New Ireland. These were not particularly productive, as by then the Japanese were more interested in cultivating their gardens to grow food than putting up any defence against enemy bombers. But the sorties did give the crews some experience, and the flights were not without incident.

Lt Clifford G Schmillen's PBJ was on a dummy strafing run when a flying fox crashed through the windscreen, showering the flight deck with animal flesh and blood.

On one sweep Lt Hamilton received a call from his wingman alerting him to the fact that the rear hatch of his aircraft was open, and that a man was standing on the extended ladder. Calling back to his crew, Hamilton asked what the hell was going on. 'It's Sanders', came the reply. 'He's sweeping out the empty cartridges. He says there are too many to unload back at base'!

Meanwhile, the attack on Rabaul continued. On 5 March all four MAG-61 PBJ units put up nearly 40 aircraft to equal many strikes by ComAirSols and Fifth Air Force a year earlier. Encountering poor weather, the formation had to fly west around New Britain prior to attacking Tobera airfield from the south at 12,000 ft. Some 20 minutes before reaching the target the port engine of Lt Max R Peterson's PBJ began to act up. On the bomb run it settled down, but the malfunction then returned, forcing Peterson to leave the formation and head for home, accompanied by Lt Howard K Horton's aircraft.

At 1130 hrs the crippled engine failed completely and the PBJ began to lose altitude. Peterson ordered all movable objects to be jettisoned. Tail gunner Cpl Charlie White unhitched his machine gun and threw it over the side, followed by ammunition boxes and, after a moment's hesitation, his parachute. At 5000 ft the PBJ stabilised and held its altitude, but then the weather deteriorated. About 50 miles from Emirau, Peterson's aircraft hit storm clouds laced with turbulence, which bought low visibility. With the radio compass out and the weather too thick for accurate navigation, Peterson had to follow Horton, who was navigating by radio compass. When they reached Emirau, Peterson circled once and made a perfect landing on one engine. Horton's PBJ followed him in.

The storm also affected the rest of VMB-611 returning from Rabaul. They dispersed on the colonel's order as visibility was too poor for formation flying. Low on fuel, Lt McRobert was given permission to land first. Lts Stanley W Kronick and Doit L Fish also managed to get down before the airfield became so socked in that Sarles and Lt Good had to detour and put down at Momote Field, in the Western Admiralties.

And that turned out to be VMB-611's last mission against Rabaul. On 7 March the unit was officially transferred to Col Jerome's MAG-32, which was then beginning the move to Mindanao. PBJ crews were first given rotational leave in Sydney, Sarles directing the stripping-down of a PBJ to carry up to ten men for the 'health and recreation' run to Australia. Not everyone got to go, as on 28 March the unit got final orders to leave for the Philippines.

Meanwhile, the early PBJ squadrons continued their night harassment war against Rabaul and associated targets from the original bases on

PBJ-1D 'Black '28', equipped with belly-mounted radar, serves as the backdrop for its assigned crew. The similarity in aircraft markings in the squadrons attached to MAG-61 often makes positive unit identification difficult, although this PBJ is almost certainly a VMB-413 machine (*Herb Lentsch*)

More 500-lb grief rains down on the long-suffering Japanese defenders of Rabaul as VMB-413 carries out another daylight raid in 1945. At least five aircraft in this formation have 'hose nose' radar, and all bear the signs of continual service (*Robert MIllington Collection*)

Stirling and Green Islands. Encounters between Japanese fighters and Marine PBJs were fairly frequent, although more often than not they ended inconclusively.

One such mission was flown by five VMB-423 PBJ-1s on 9 June 1944. Its purpose was, to quote the aircraft action report, 'harass the Rabaul area and search and attack any enemy aircraft encountered'. Each PBJ carried six 100-lb GP bombs, which were to be dropped on the airstrips at Tobera, Lakunai and Vunakanau, with some reserved for what was simply described in the report as a 'light (almost certainly a searchlight) near Vunakanau strip'.

Using call signs '40-B-22' to '44-B-22', the Mitchells, piloted by Hopper, Ivie, B M Jones, Lusky and Eckhardt, departed Stirling Island at 1455 hrs and landed on Green Island at 1613 hrs in preparation for a target take off time of 1730 hrs. Time on target for the first PBJ was to be from 1800 to 2045 hrs.

At 1810 hrs Hopper dropped the first 100 'pounder' on Tobera (the only one as it turned out), before proceeding to do the same at Lakunai. Although there was no reaction to the raid on the first airstrip, the PBJ stirred up a hornet's nest at the second. Heavy, but inaccurate, flak came up from the gun positions on Hospital Ridge, but there were no searchlights or interceptors. By 1840 hrs Hopper was some 10,000 ft above Vunakanau when two Ki-43 'Oscars' were sighted. The Japanese pilots looped, rolled and played around the bombers for a full five minutes, their purpose, the Americans believed, being to entice the PBJ down to a lower altitude, and thus within range of the flak gunners. Instead, the PBJ stayed at height, and the 'Oscars' climbed and made four attack runs.

It was some time before the Japanese pilots opened fire, their two passes being in the nature of probing attacks. On the third run, a high side 'S' approach was made from starboard to port, commencing at about 2000 ft above the PBJ and descending to 500 ft. The fighters then opened fire, but scored no hits after expending an estimated 200 rounds. The PBJ crew returned fire with forward and turret guns, and likewise scored no hits despite the gunners loosing off a total 650 rounds.

A fourth run by the 'Oscars' took the form of an overhead reverse, initiated some 3000 ft above the bomber. Opening fire at 1000 yards, the two enemy pilots continued firing until they dived past the PBJ at an estimated speed of 350 to 400 knots – too fast for the Marine gunners to draw a bead on them. Hopper had timed his counter move well. When the 'Oscars' were 2000 yards out, he kicked the PBJ's nose over, boosting speed from 100 to 180 knots. This manoeuvre, combined with fish-tailing, probably helped confuse the enemy pilots as to both range and deflection – much of their expended 5000 rounds apiece passed harmlessly between the PBJ's wing and tail.

At 1855 hrs both fighters, later reported by the Marines to be well handled, circled down until they were lost in cloud at some 6000 ft. The

Demonstrating the enemy's respect for downed aircrew, Ken Meyer (far left) points out the holes made in this dinghy by Japanese machine gun bullets after his PBJ was shot down. The VMB-423 crew rescued after eight hours adrift were, standing, from left to right, S W Carlson, Jim Cameron and Eddie Leonard, and kneeling, from left to right, Dick Voss, Tony Mezzelo and Dale Harris (*Robert Millington Collection*)

PBJ pilot believed that they broke off the engagement so as to land before dark. With the fighters gone, the flak batteries opened up, but none of the small attacking force reported any damage. All bombed their objectives, and the first aircraft was back at Green Island by 2125 hrs. All participating PBJs returned safely.

CLOSE CALL

On 30 October 1944 a VMB-423 PBJ was hit by automatic fire and the pilot, 1Lt Kenneth G Meyer, was forced to ditch in St George's Channel, off Rabaul. The PBJ-1D, coded '38', was put down well enough for the crew to clamber into a life raft. After eight hours afloat, the men were picked up by a PBY. Back at Green Island, they showed off the raft to a Corps photographer, complete with patches over holes made by Japanese small arms that had been fired at them while they were in the water.

During December VMB-423 began a training programme designed to increase close support capability. This continued into January 1945, and the squadron carried on much as before with missions to New Britain and New Ireland. New pilots and crews were also given theatre training, and members of the MAG-61 PBJ units soon realised they were not going anywhere. They came to accept that they were fighting a largely forgotten war, and that all they had to do was keep the enemy from breaking out of their blockaded bases to satisfy McArthur's strategy, and the original Marine Corps plan for deploying PBJs as night 'hecklers'.

The Japanese had occupied part of Bougainville since March 1942, and in November 1943 US forces landed in Empress Augusta Bay.

On Green Island on 25 November 1944, the Marines celebrated the first PBJ to complete 100 missions – this honour fell to a VMB-423 aircraft attached to MAW-1. The Mitchell's war scars reflect the dedication of the groundcrew to keep it flying. They are, front row, from left to right, Cpls Raymond E Lawrence and George Wadle and Sgt Joseph W Cope, centre row, from left to right, Cpl Robert D Deemer and Pfc Charles E Dillow, and back row, from left to right, Sgt Robert D Lee, S/Sgt Leon P Peterson (Crew Chief) and Cpl Fred Jaroslowsky (*USMC*)

After fending off counter-attacks, the American troops consolidated their position, leaving both sides to predominantly remain in their enclaves for the next 12 months. Not until November 1944 did things change when the Australians decided to secure the entire island. Air support was provided by RAAF, RNZAF and US squadrons, the latter including Marine PBJs.

On 6 February 1945, Maj John T Pritchard led seven PBJs on a medium altitude bombing raid on Muguai, Bougainville, this operation being carefully coordinated with RNZAF Corsairs based at Piva, on the southern coast. The Australian Army was by then in the process of capturing the island, and had requested a concentration of high explosive on a Japanese tank park at Ruri. The Marines obliged by placing seven bombs in the designated target area. The ground fighting on Bougainville reached a peak between 28 March and 6 April 1945, when the Australians beat off several Japanese attacks. After taking heavy losses, the enemy withdrew. Allied air strikes, thereafter, contained them until war's end.

April brought a spell of good flying weather, enabling VMB-423 to concentrate its bombing efforts on Bougainville. ComAirNorSols relieved the squadron of operational responsibilities elsewhere in the South Pacific, with the result that 35 medium bombing, 11 low-level bombing and strafing and 20 night 'heckling' missions were carried out. In addition, VMB-423 mounted three photo-reconnaissance and seven search missions during the month. Still led by Lt Col Norman Anderson, the unit relocated to Emirau on 12 June – it remained here until August 1945, when it moved to Malabang.

Having spent most of its operational time at Emirau, VMB-423's sister-squadron VMB-433 did not suffer any fatalities until 2 September 1944, when the PBJ piloted by Lts Charles L Ingels and Richard R Graves was lost with four other crew, including one passenger.

The unit was to lose another aircraft later that month when 1Lt Eric E Terry Jr went down after being hit by flak. Two crewmen were picked up by a Dumbo PBY, but the pilot and navigator and the two remaining crew members were lost. One man was killed in action on 4 December in unknown circum-

When VMB-612's PBJs dropped most of their machine guns to save weight on long over-water flights, the squadron's favoured armament became the high velocity aircraft rocket (HVAR). Each PBJ carried eight, and armourers are seen here checking rockets with shaped-charge heads (*via Thomas Honeycutt*)

Probably snapped from the waist position of a sister-ship PBJ-1D, 'Black 40' releases its 500 'pounders' over the Gazelle Peninsula in early 1945. The Mitchell's parent unit was probably VMB-413 (*via Alan Carey*)

stances, and VMB-433's last combat loss came on 27 February 1945 when 1Lt Donald R Harpley and his crew of five went down.

VMB-433 then experienced a series of command changes that did little to boost morale in a wartime backwater. On 2 April the original CO was replaced by Lt Col Winton H Miller, who stayed for just a month until Maj Boyd O Whitney took over. Neither individuals was able to instill much confidence in the squadron, and it was not until 17 July, when Lt Col Andrew G Smith Jr assumed command, that the unit regained its equilibrium. Under 'Guy' Smith, VMB-433 continued to operate from Emirau until VJ-Day, and in August it joined other PBJ units in the Philippines in the penultimate step to decommissioning on 30 November 1945.

By the spring of 1945 it was clear to all concerned that the shooting war in the South Pacific was taking second place to training, tedious search missions and weather reconnaissance sorties by American airmen, while the Japanese battled desperately to sustain men all but cut off from their supplies. The worst aspect for the PBJ squadrons were the occasional crew losses and the difficulty of integrating officers fresh out of flight school. Some of these individuals were looking merely to log flight time in a combat zone, and thus had more confidence than ability. Their antics at the controls of a PBJ could scare the hell out of veterans who had lived through some tough situations, and who wanted to continue doing so.

On 11 September 1944 VMB-443, which also continued to fly from Emirau, recorded that Lt John O'Hara's crew had failed to return from an escort trip to Talasea, New Britain. None of the six-man crew survived.

Six days later the squadron participated in the first large-scale PBJ anti-shipping strike in the South Pacific. During this operation, which was to support Fifth Air Force covering the US landings on Moratai, Palau, Ulithi and Peleliu, the aircraft crewed by 1Lts Benjamin G Kinnack, Dominic F Bellanca and four enlisted men went down and was lost. Two days later 1Lt John L Braden was forced to ditch a PBJ, and he and M/Sgt Gerald N Griffith perished. The other members of the crew were rescued.

ENTER VMB-612

As a semi-official history of the unit states, VMB-612 was the most unusual Marine Corps squadron to operate in the Central Pacific, and it owed its origins to the Japanese success in the early days of the

PBJs believed to have been from VMB-433 sweep off a target on Matupi Island, which is still belching smoke in the left centre background (*Robert Millington Collection*)

With bombs exploding on Vunakanau airfield in the background, a pair of PBJ-1Ds of VMB-433 turn for home on 5 January 1945 to chalk up another successful sortie against Rabaul (*Robert Millington Collection*)

Solomons campaign. Then, the Imperial Navy's notorious nocturnal runs down the 'Slot' to replenish its shore-based troops and pour fire onto US defences had almost tipped the balance. Determined not to be caught out by a repeat performance, Navy chiefs urged the formation of three squadrons trained and equipped to operate at night with radar and other special detection devices. Two of these were Navy units flying Venturas and PB4Y Liberators and the third was Lt Col Jack Cram's VMB-612.

Commissioned at Cherry Point on 1 October 1943, VMB-612 was originally intended as a conventional PBJ day bombing outfit, but in February 1944 it was chosen for experimental work in low altitude night bombing using radar. Assembling such a squadron was not without its problems. For one thing, there was a shortage of personnel, although men steadily trickled into Cherry Point alongside a full compliment of PBJ-1Cs and Ds. One 'green 18-year-old radar technician with no experience' attached to VMB-612 was Bill Bessinger. He reported for duty and was immediately put to work modifying the unit's PBJs. He recalled;

'Our training had not extended to installation of equipment in aircraft. I knew nothing of naval aviation regulations. A R Wilson (a staff NCO with radar knowledge) and I were setting out to modify and install gear in 15 aeroplanes – a project that grew until 48 had been modified. Our headquarters was the A&R hanger. It became my world for 16 to 20 hours each day. Work was done around the clock. To install new gear, the old gear had to be removed. Where we put the gear we had, and where to leave room for the anticipated gear, was the next problem. The APS-3 radar dome went in the nose because it was thought to have less (detrimental) effect on the flight characteristics in that location, and also the cable runs that a wing installation would have demanded would have been excessive.

'The APQ-5 bombing gear was set up to operate from the bombardier's position in the nose because that was the normal location for him on a run. There was plenty of space in the nose, and the search gear and radios (including the 720 interrogator-responder set) were located so as to be as convenient as possible for the operator. The IFF gear, which required no regular attention, was put where space permitted. Anything else went where we could squeeze it in.'

Lt Col Jack Cram was VMB-612's energetic leader from November 1943 until February 1945. A Marine with considerable flying experience, Cram had previously been commended for some hazardous flying at the controls of a PBY. His PBJ unit adopted the nickname 'Cram's Rams' to reflect both the quality of his leadership and the esteem in which he was held (*North American Aviation*)

For the final period of the war VMB-612's PBJs wore the overall sea blue colour scheme introduced for patrol bombers in 1944. In this view, a crane assists the groundcrew as they change an engine at Boca Chica prior to the unit heading overseas (*via Thomas Honeycutt*)

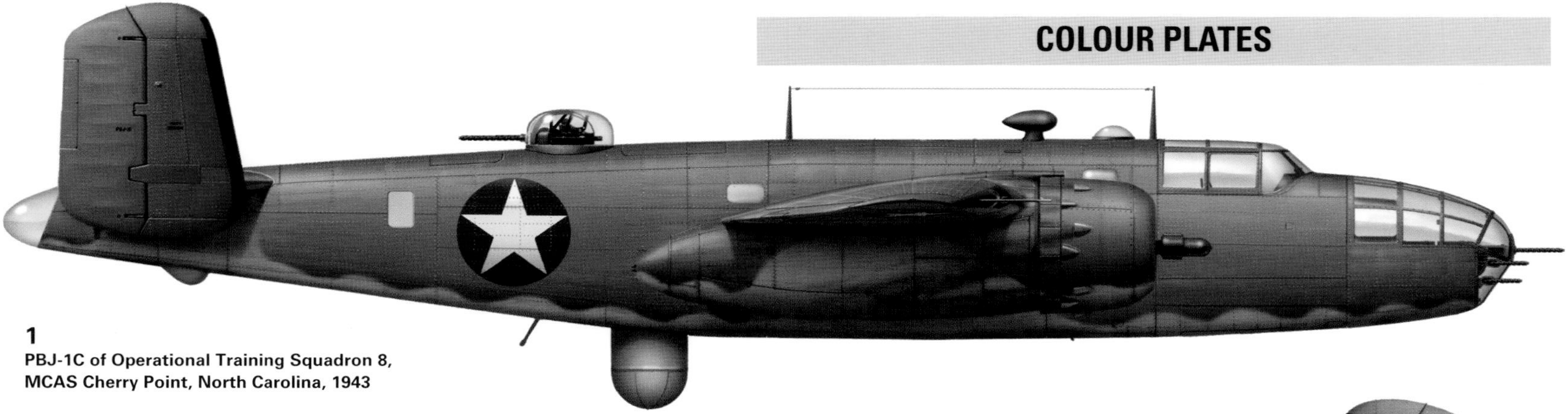

1
PBJ-1C of Operational Training Squadron 8,
MCAS Cherry Point, North Carolina, 1943

2
PBJ-1D BuNo 35094 *JONAH*,
MCAS Cherry Point,
North Carolina, 1944

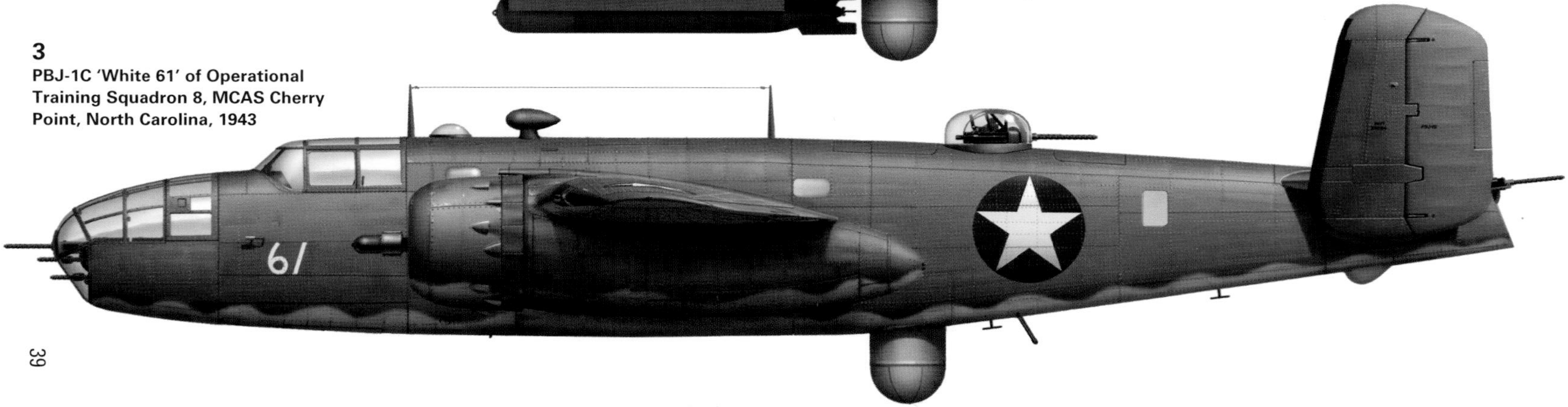

3
PBJ-1C 'White 61' of Operational
Training Squadron 8, MCAS Cherry
Point, North Carolina, 1943

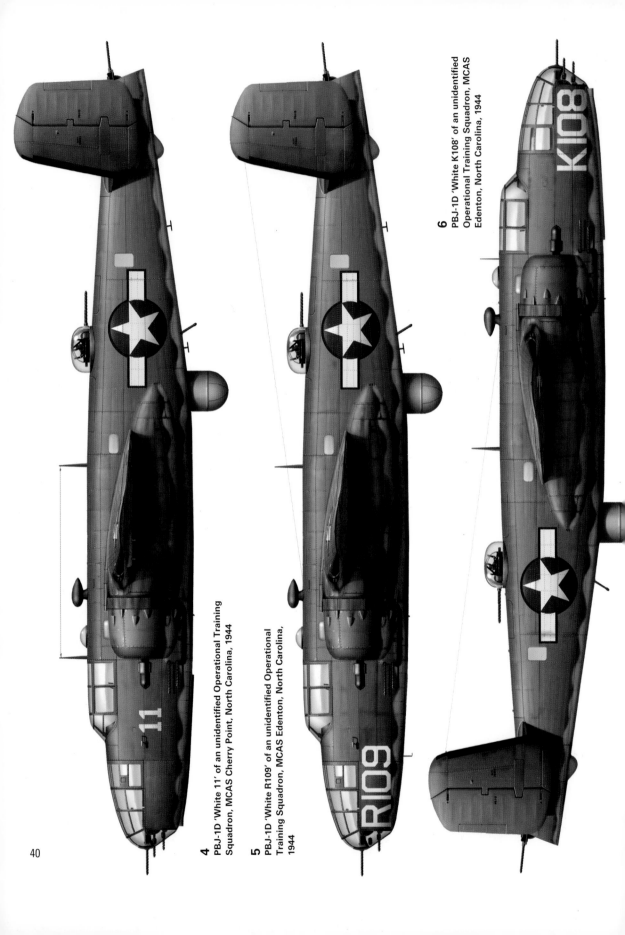

4
PBJ-1D 'White 11' of an unidentified Operational Training Squadron, MCAS Cherry Point, North Carolina, 1944

5
PBJ-1D 'White R109' of an unidentified Operational Training Squadron, MCAS Edenton, North Carolina, 1944

6
PBJ-1D 'White K108' of an unidentified Operational Training Squadron, MCAS Edenton, North Carolina, 1944

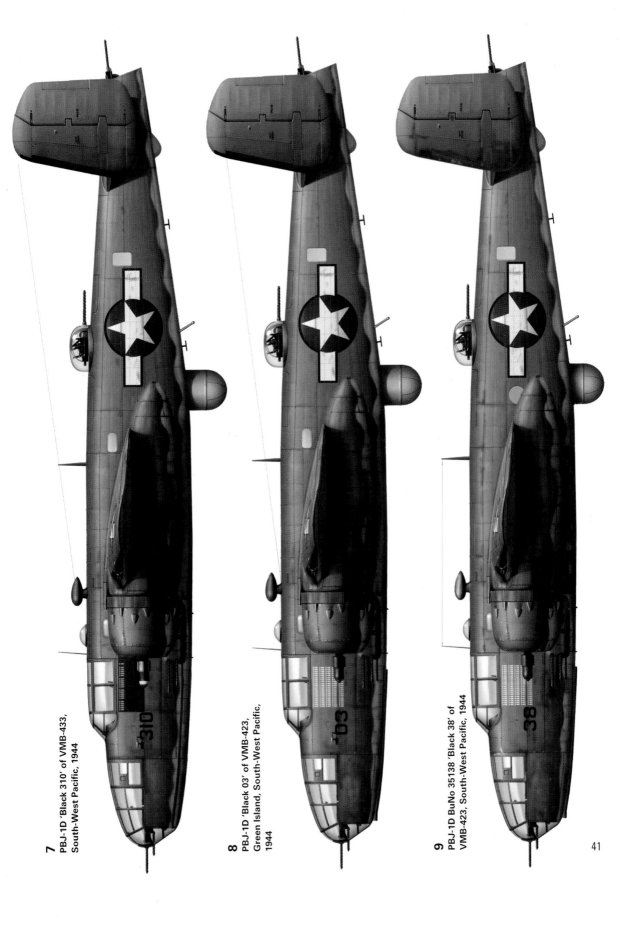

7
PBJ-1D 'Black 310' of VMB-433,
South-West Pacific, 1944

8
PBJ-1D 'Black 03' of VMB-423,
Green Island, South-West Pacific,
1944

9
PBJ-1D BuNo 35138 'Black 38' of
VMB-423, South-West Pacific, 1944

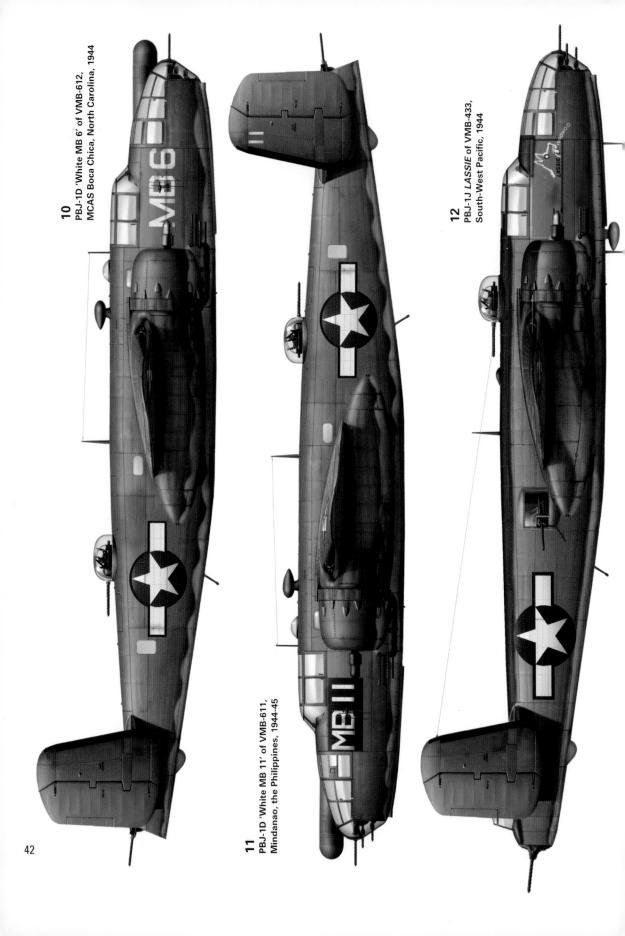

10
PBJ-1D 'White MB 6' of VMB-612,
MCAS Boca Chica, North Carolina, 1944

11
PBJ-1D 'White MB 11' of VMB-611,
Mindanao, the Philippines, 1944-45

12
PBJ-1J *LASSIE* of VMB-433,
South-West Pacific, 1944

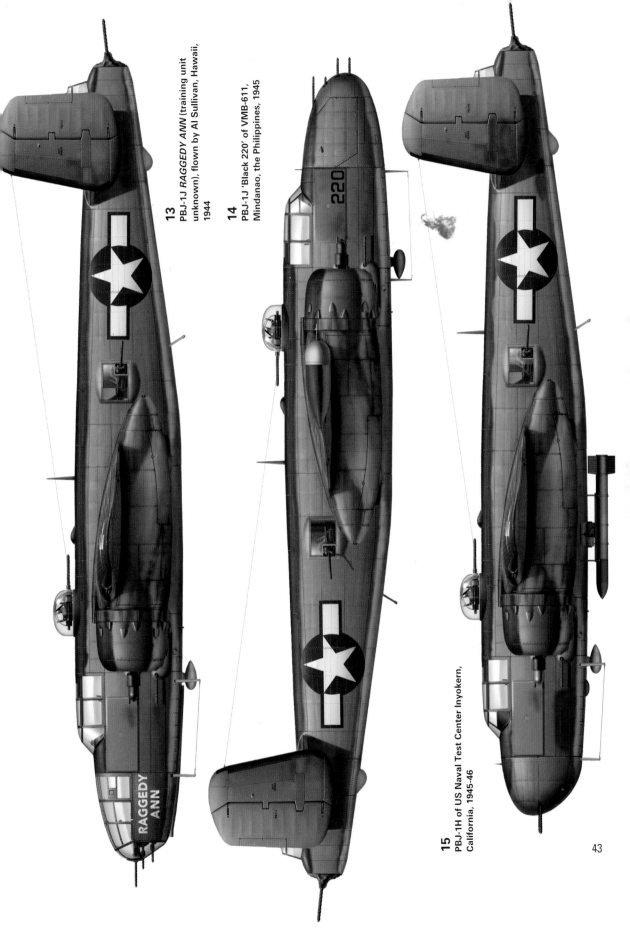

13
PBJ-1J *RAGGEDY ANN* (training unit
unknown), flown by Al Sullivan, Hawaii,
1944

14
PBJ-1J 'Black 220' of VMB-611,
Mindanao, the Philippines, 1945

15
PBJ-1H of US Naval Test Center Inyokern,
California, 1945-46

43

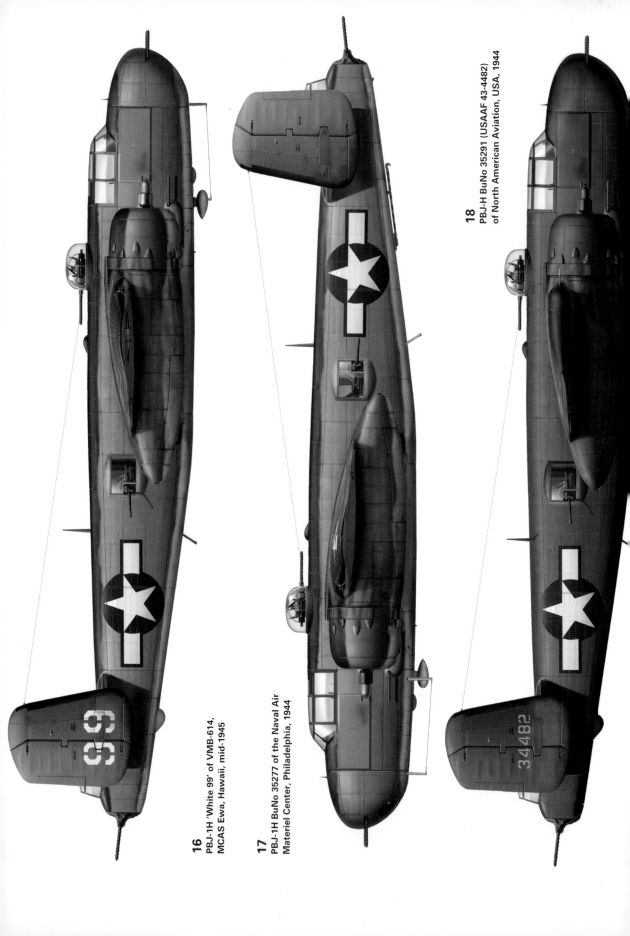

16
PBJ-1H 'White 99' of VMB-614,
MCAS Ewa, Hawaii, mid-1945

17
PBJ-1H BuNo 35277 of the Naval Air
Materiel Center, Philadelphia, 1944

18
PBJ-H BuNo 35291 (USAAF 43-4482)
of North American Aviation, USA, 1944

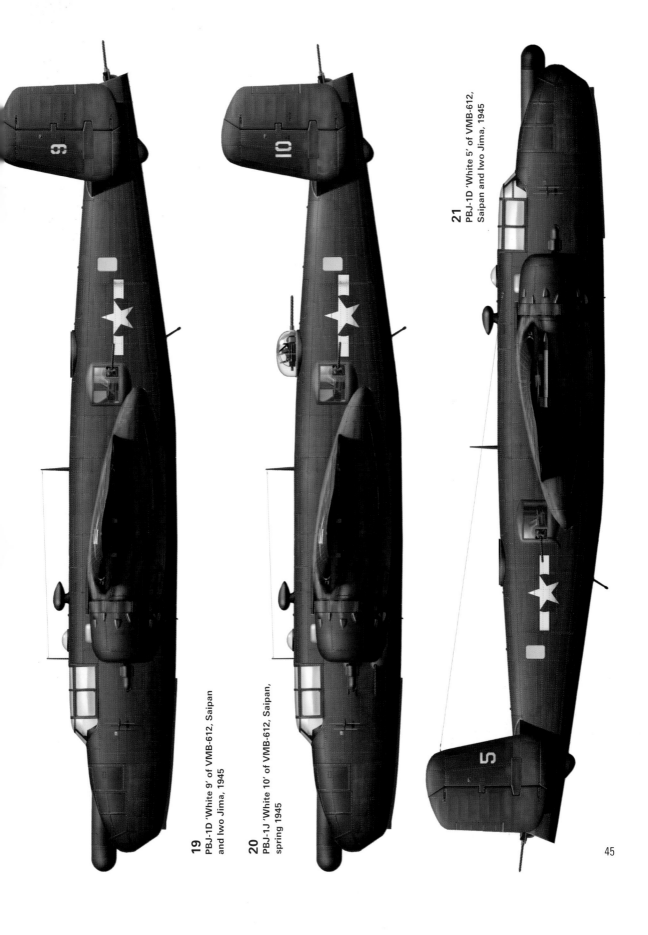

19
PBJ-1D 'White 9' of VMB-612, Saipan
and Iwo Jima, 1945

20
PBJ-1J 'White 10' of VMB-612, Saipan,
spring 1945

21
PBJ-1D 'White 5' of VMB-612,
Saipan and Iwo Jima, 1945

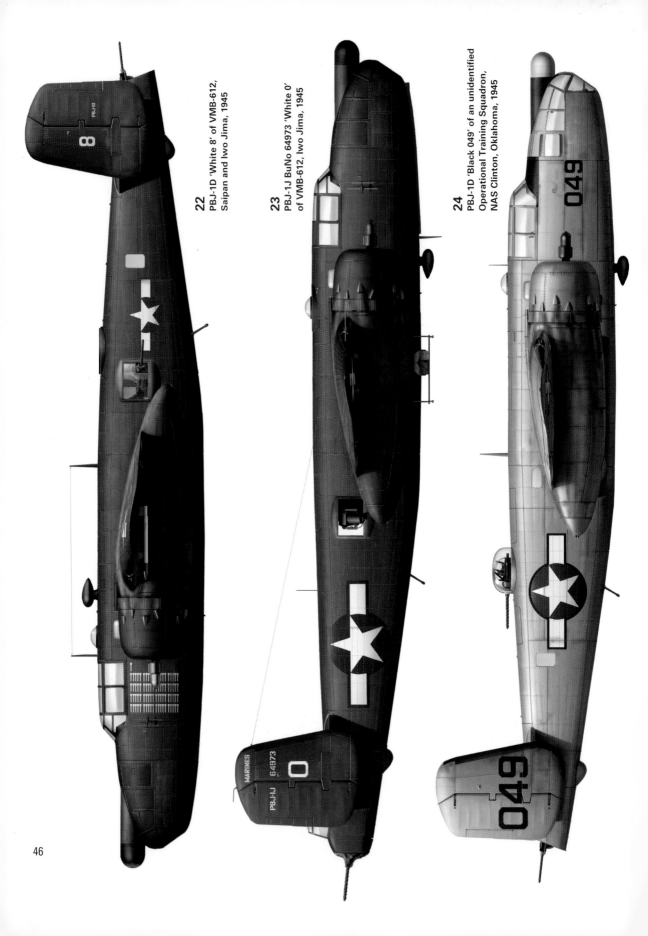

22
PBJ-1D 'White 8' of VMB-612,
Saipan and Iwo Jima, 1945

23
PBJ-1J BuNo 64973 'White 0'
of VMB-612, Iwo Jima, 1945

24
PBJ-1D 'Black 049' of an unidentified
Operational Training Squadron,
NAS Clinton, Oklahoma, 1945

SUNDAY PUNCH

On 9 April 1945 the US Army's 10th Corps, comprising the 24th and 31st Infantry Divisions, landed on the west coast of Mindanao, in the Philippines, and proceeded to fight its way across the island to Davao. The 41st Division, meanwhile, landed to the north at Jolo. Maj Gen Ralph Mitchell had overall command of Marine air units in the southern Philippines campaign, comprising Marine Air Groups 12 and 14 with 85 F4Us, and Marine Air Groups 24 and 32 with 192 SBDs. VMB-611 had 16 PBJs, which became part of Marine Air Group Zamboanga (MAGSZAM) under Col Clayton Jerome. Its task was to support 10th Corps for the duration of the campaign.

The task of Marine airpower was to deploy SBD Dauntless dive-bombers and F4U Corsair fighter-bombers in direct support of the ground forces in their drive across the Philippines in the face of expected heavy opposition. Harder targets, including enemy headquarters, artillery, defensive positions, airfields and fortified areas, were to be 'softened up' and attacked day and night by VMB-611's PBJs. Their radar and long-range radio, plus comprehensive navigational aids including Loran, were considered particularly valuable. In training VMB-611, the Marines had placed great emphasis on night flying, leading the crews to believe that they would be flying mostly nocturnal missions. In the Philippines, however, this was generally not to be the case.

On 15 March 1945 the VMB-611 groundcrews finally headed for dry land by LST, bidding the *Loella Lykes* a none-too-fond farewell. They had by then become part of the supply fleet for the Mindanao invasion, and as such were bound for Moret Field, outside Zamboanga City.

Masters of concealment, the 58,000 Japanese troops on Mindanao would, on past performance, have to be forcibly ejected from every foxhole, pillbox and house before the Philippines could be recaptured. Houses, in the Western sense, were relatively new targets for the airborne Marines, but with the capital Manila firmly under Japanese control, ground troops found house-by-house fighting developing virtually for the first time in the Pacific war. Taking the city became a protracted, bloody affair that could so easily have been avoided had the wise council of the Japanese Army commander (the late Gen Orimoto) been heeded. Instead, troops went on a bloody spree, which had unfortunate consequences both for the Japanese and the civilian inhabitants of the city.

In preparation for operations from Moret Field, VMB-611 groundcrews set up shop in a coconut grove adjoining the airstrip and the aircraft arrived on 30 March. Initial operations were to the Sulu Islands, 85 miles to the south, where one regiment of the 41st Division was engaged in capturing airfield sites from which the Thirteenth Air Force could support the Australian invasion of Borneo. This operation, which went ahead despite the 41st's main preoccupation with driving the Japanese out of Zamboanga, needed all the air support the PBJs could provide. Col Sarles led the first strike, a night bombing mission with a four-ship flight.

Carrying 32 250-lb bombs and 32 five-inch rockets, the PBJs were briefed to pound troop and artillery concentrations south of Bongao town near the beach on the island of the same name. Darkness and low cloud greeted the Marine aircrews, who made a radar approach. Sarles dropped a flare, and although several bombing runs were made, the light was not sufficient for a satisfactory attack. The following day nine PBJs made a medium altitude horizontal bombing run and placed a pattern of 32 500-lb bombs into the troop and gun positions. Results were described as excellent.

Two nights later the PBJs returned to the Bongao beach-head. This time four of the aircraft carried a single one-million candlepower flare on their lower bomb-bay racks. The flight leader dropped his flare first while the second PBJ came in to bomb and rocket the target before dropping his flare. The third aircraft bombed on the flare dropped by the second and so on. At dawn the landing forces hit the beach and waded ashore without any casualties, enabling VMB-611 to turn its attention to Jolo, the largest island in the archipelago and the next scheduled for invasion. The PBJs then spent several days attacking artillery positions and the road leading from the beach, their rocket and bomb strikes creating safe conditions for US forces who went ashore on 8 April, again without casualties. In all these operations, close support was provided by Marine Dauntlesses.

VMB-611's final operation in the Sulus was on 9 April, by which time the 163rd Regimental Combat Team had pushed the Japanese back to the base of Mount Daho, where they intended to mount a last ditch defence. A large bunker formed the centrepiece of a defensive line that stretched about a third of a mile, flanked by a complex of rocks, ravines and caves. Throwing themselves against these fortifications would have caused unnecessary US casualties, so the Marine PBJs were called in.

Although 33 Marine SBDs were also available, they could not dive-bomb effectively because of the close proximity of steep cliffs. Horizontal precision bombing using the Norden sight was required. The PBJs responded with widely-spaced individual runs, dropping 1000-lb bombs. One of these hit the main bunker and demolished it, while others fell among the adjoining positions. The SBDs then assaulted the broken defensive line, while the PBJs made rocket attacks. When the position was taken, a Marine air-liaison offer reported that about half the estimated 400 defending Japanese had been killed in the air strikes.

At this time VMB-611 PBJ-1C/Ds were as standard as any Marine Mitchell could be said to be. Then squadron groundcrews added a further modification which was also seen on some VMB-612 aircraft, and was believed to be unique to the early models. The large 'bay' windows situated just aft of the wing on each side of the fuselage of the

Several PBJs racked up impressive mission totals, and crews duly recorded them in small bomb silhouettes as had become a wartime tradition. While frowning on garish names and artwork, the Marine Corps did permit bomb logs to be painted on aircraft. PBJ-1D 'Black 26' has 21 missions recorded (*Herb Lentsch*)

C/D models held a 0.50-cal machine gun and provided excellent visibility for the gunner, but they were also vulnerable. A gunner or crewmen standing at the windows was at risk if enemy fire hit the aircraft during a low-level attack run. Sheet metal shops therefore 'boarded up' the windows so that only a small observation slit and a slot to allow the gun to traverse remained. Several of VMB-611's PBJ-1Cs boasted such a modification during Zamboanga operations, and they were also seen on VMB-612's PBJ-1Cs on Iwo Jima.

MINDANAO

In early April, while 10th Corps was occupied in the Sulus, Col Wendell Fertig decided to send a guerrilla force of about 150 Moros and Filipinos to capture Malabang airfield, situated on the eastern side of the Moro Gulf from Zamboanga. It had been abandoned by the enemy, and Fertig wanted to secure it while he had the chance. Assigning Australian Maj Blow to the task, Fertig soon got word that the airfield had been secured. Too late the Japanese realised Malabang would be a thorn in their side, and opted to send about 650 troops to flush the guerrillas out. With no 10th Corps troops able to help, and the SBDs occupied at Jolo, only VMB-611's PBJs could provide air support.

Col Sarles immediately added Malabang to his target list as part of the campaign to secure eastern Mindanao. He led six PBJs across the Moro Gulf on 7 April, the aircraft arriving over the beach area armed with depth charges. Each PBJ could carry three 300-lb charges per side on its two wing racks, but the total load deployed on this occasion is unrecorded. Flying up the Malabang River at 1500 ft, the PBJs came upon a large, grassy pasture. A Jeep was parked on the edge with Blow aboard, waving. Radio contact could not be made with the bombers, so Sarles decided to land in the pasture, with Lt Hoadley's aircraft following suit. Delighted to see the PBJs, the guerrillas materialised from the undergrowth.

Summing up the situation, Sarles ordered Hoadley to stay on the ground and use his radio to maintain an air-ground link and talk the bombers to their targets just across the river. The colonel then took off to join the other four circling PBJs. They came in at tree-top level, widely spaced in line-astern. Each PBJ dropped four depth charges which exploded, creating shock waves and mind-blowing concussion. When the PBJs had left the guerrillas simply crossed the river and finished off the stunned enemy survivors.

Sarles and his small unit landed at Malabang to plan further strikes for the following day. It was decided to attack positions along the shoreline and immediately inland from the beach, where the Japanese had prepared defensive positions. Hoadley made 8 April a field day. His crew dropped six bombs along a Japanese trench line, knocked out three machine gun nests with rockets and destroyed three buildings occupied by the enemy. As a finale, the PBJ bombed a radio shack and strafed the area, before returning to Moret Field.

Other PBJs followed up the initial strikes, placing a total of 23 bombs on troop concentrations and machine gun nests along the banks of the Malabang River before strafing the area. In the afternoon, Blow became an air controller from the seat of an L-5. He led the PBJs, flown by Maj Prescott Fagan and Lts Mason, Good and Samuels, to finish off the remaining enemy positions. This broke the back of the defences and the Japanese withdrew that night.

BUKIDNON VALLEY

With Malabang secure VMB-611 turned its attention to Gen Morozumi's 30th Division in the Bukidnon Valley in north central Mindanao, which runs for about 100 miles between two mountain ranges from Macajalar Bay in the north then south along the Sayre road to Kibawe. Morozumi's first line of defence was a patch of high ground some eight miles inland. A natural defensive feature, it covered any approach from the sea. This high ground included Del Monte airfield, captured by the Japanese in 1941 and since extended. Supply flights came in at night and the airfield was well defended. There were no fighters but plenty of flak batteries. These were to pose the biggest danger to the PBJs, as the gunners did not use tracer rounds. Crews returning to base found holes in their aircraft that they believed, at first, to have been made by the blast of their own bombs.

Bukidnon Valley became VMB-611's personal hunting ground for ten days in early April because the SBDs were still supporting the 41st Division. There were three reasons for concentrating PBJ attacks in the valley: US air activity served as a feint to make the Japanese believe Allied troops would land at Macajalar Bay instead of Parang; the defences in the valley would be softened up before friendly troops reached it; and Del Monte airfield could be neutralised.

Initially, Lt John Coons led two PBJs on a reconnaissance sweep of the valley along the Sayre road, before finishing up with a glance at Del Monte. Japanese flak opened up just as Coons crossed the airfield boundary, shells blowing away most of his right rudder and wounding Pfc Bill Olsen. Coons maintained control, called the other PBJ in to escort him home and eventually landed safely.

On 10 April Sarles opened his campaign with a six-aeroplane strike on Del Monte airfield, and surrounding troop positions, to be led by Maj Fagan. The PBJs were to go in at low-level using 250-lb bombs and rockets. Flight crews breakfasted on Spam, bread and coffee and picked up their Thermos flasks of coffee before making their way to trucks to take them out to their bombers. Each man carried a flying jacket, although a low-level sortie over the Philippines did not require the heavy clothing that a higher altitude mission would have done. Jumping off the trucks at their assigned aircraft, each six-man crew clambered aboard, three using the PBJs' front hatches and three the rear ones.

Once aboard, it was soon time to go. Crew chiefs signalled engine start, and as Fagan's aircraft lifted off, the other five followed to form up into a loose 'V of Vs'. Course was set across the gulf towards Moro and Lake Lanao. Radiomen checked their frequencies, while turret gunners broke out the coffee. Pilots maintained a loose formation as their co-pilots scanned the instruments and navigators logged wind drift.

At the coast the small formation changed course at Malabang so as to pass north of Lake Lanao on their approach to Del Monte. Fagan led his force down to 3000 ft and circled the airfield to come in out of the sun. Seeing a truck racing up the dirt road towards the plateau, Fagan dropped down and gave it a long burst from his seven forward-firing guns. As the truck went off the road the other pilots tested their fixed guns on it. Then all hell broke loose. The Japanese had positioned flak batteries on the same side of the plateau as Del Monte airfield. Spotting the guns only by their muzzle flashes, the PBJ crews came around and blasted every one they could identify with machine guns, rockets and bombs. The navigator usually got off the first shots from his free nose gun as the PBJ banked round to line up on the gun pits. Then the pilots dropped bombs or fired wing rockets. Finally the turret and tail gunners each got off a few bursts.

Fagan did not loiter long over the gun emplacements. With his force intact, he led a pass down the runway and destroyed a Ki-45 'Nick' parked in a revetment. Turning south, the PBJs laid a bomb carpet on a troop concentration previously noted on a reconnaissance photograph. Continuing, the PBJs swept the slopes of the plateau for any installations they could find, before making a final pass down the nearby road.

A few days later photo-reconnaissance brought back evidence of camouflaged buildings identified by guerrillas as warehouses and barracks. This was clearly a ripe target, but a medium altitude strike from 8000 ft would be problematical. Lt Raymond B Taylor, senior officer of the PBJ navigator-bombardiers, voiced his concern that by the time the buildings came clearly into view, and were lined up in the crosshairs, the bombardiers would have to toggle the load very rapidly at that altitude, probably compromising accuracy. But orders were orders, and Taylor's opinion was ignored. A six-aeroplane mission, with the PBJs carrying a maximum load of four 1000-lb bombs each, went off the following day. All it achieved were near misses. Sarles sent the same six crews out again that afternoon, this time arming the PBJs with 250-lb bombs. This attack was more successful, but at some cost to the unit.

Lt Charlie Good was in the first of two sections to bomb, and the buildings were duly pulverised. Good and his co-pilot, Lt Clayton, then spotted a Japanese aircraft in a revetment and decided to strafe it. Circling back towards the runway for the run, the PBJ was targeted by an anti-aircraft gun crew. Suddenly, a 37 mm shell slammed into the bomber's left engine and knocked it out. A second shell exploded in the navigator's compartment, setting hydraulic fluid on fire and wounding Clayton in the thigh. Fortunately, the navigator, S/Sgt Jack LeFevour, was in the nose at the time blazing away with his front gun. Realising the ship was hit, he

While VMB-612 was operating in the central Pacific, MAG-61 squadrons continued to pound away at the bypassed islands in the South-West Pacific while the training squadrons fed fresh crew replacements as required. This PBJ-1D, with the black nose code '24', was photographed on a training sortie over desolate scrubland

hauled himself back to his compartment, grabbed an extinguisher and put out the fire. LeFevour then attended to Clayton's leg.

In the meantime, Good was losing the battle to keep the crippled PBJ in the air, and he called for the crew to throw out anything moveable to lighten the aircraft. Heading for Lake Lanoa or the ocean to ditch, Good tried his best, but one of the Mitchell's wings sheared off the top of a tree, kicking the wing upwards and slamming the fuselage down against a hillside. The PBJ bounced and slid to a crashing halt, the rear section breaking and slewing round at a 90-degree angle.

Despite wounds ranging from serious burns – the PBJ exploded soon after the crew escaped – to slight concussion, none of the crew fell into enemy hands as Good had come down near a guerrilla headquarters. They were later picked up by a PBY and flown to Zamboanga, but Pfc Barney Allen succumbed to terrible burns received when he was trapped in the wrecked aircraft. After Good's PBJ went down the third flight also suffered as a result of the concealed flak battery. A shell explode above the cockpit of Lt Lauer's PBJ, showering both him and co-pilot Lt Klockzien with glass fragments. Both men were sufficiently incapacitated for Lt Taylor, the navigator-bombardier, to take over and fly back to Moret Field, where he performed a successful landing.

For the next week VMB-612 pounded the valley area, dropping 500-lb bombs on the airfield from 8000 ft before going in low to strafe and rocket road transport, supplies, gun positions and enemy troops. One mission was to destroy an ammunition dump hidden in Mother Lode Mine, which was located in a small, steep-sided canyon, making it difficult to spot from the air.

Although the PBJs tried horizontal bombing and low-level gun and rocket attacks, the mine and adjacent warehouses proved almost impossible to hit. Col Sarles then called in a guerrilla unit. By setting up a radio in sight of the mine, the guerrilla leader could talk the bombers right over the target. Sarles and his wingman, Lt Schmillen, proved once again that a small force could achieve much. Circling the canyon to draw Japanese fire, Sarles gave Schmillen's navigator, S/Sgt Chester Hodun, a direct line in. Two 1000-lb bombs went straight into the mine shaft entrance and demolished the warehouses.

On 17 April the 24th Division went ashore at Parang, taking the Japanese completely by surprise. There was no opposition until intelligence revealed a small enemy unit at Cotobato, a small town up the Mindanao River. As this was to be an amphibious assault point for US troops, four PBJs were sent in along with SBDs. The job was done in short order.

Light relief for the Marine Mitchell crews in the Philippines could hardly be described as frequent, or lavish, but entertainers did reach their far-flung outposts from time to time. Comedian Joe E Brown not only visited VMB-611 at this time, but begged to fly on the 17 April mission with George Sarles. Brown's son had recently been killed, and he probably wished to see some of the action his boy had been involved in. The Marines had nothing but praise and admiration for the 54-year-old comedian's spirit under trying circumstances.

Despite the delay caused by the enemy demolition of adjacent bridges, Malabang was open for business by 22 April. MAG-24 soon moved in, but was not immediately operational. A mission for VMB-611 was scheduled for that day after it became known that Gen Morozumi had moved reinforcements into the Bukidnon Valley to await advancing American forces. The Marine mediums were briefed to attack along the valley road from Malaybalay to Kabacan. Sarles sent the by now customary four pairs of bombers by day and three singles by night. Road transport, artillery positions, an observation post and depots were hit with guns and rockets during the daylight sorties. At night, Valencia was shot up and what had become Highway 1 was subjected to flare illumination which revealed a column of 30+ Japanese trucks. Two PBJs received flak hits and one caught debris from a rocket blast, but there were no casualties.

On 23 April the 31st Division began to disembark troops at Parang, while the 2nd Battalion, 124th Infantry Regiment was obliged to travel up the Mindanao River and force-march to Kabacan. Late that evening they came under fire from the Japanese. Digging in, the American troops endured a night banzai charge. Meanwhile, the 3rd Battalion was forced to haul equipment over difficult terrain to offset the fact that the enemy had blown every available bridge from Kabacan to Kibawe. Making a supreme effort to cross a high canyon held by the enemy, Gen Eichelberger's men surprised the Japanese by improvising, using little more than basic climbing skills.

During this campaign VMB-611 flew supporting night patrols, shooting up what road transport it could find. Such action caused the Japanese to turn off their vehicle lights and melt into the jungle, making them almost impossible to detect from the air. But progress was being made on the ground, despite the enemy being well aware of US intentions to capture Maramag airfield, and building his defences accordingly. The area held plenty of natural cover, so it was decided to bypass these formidable positions and capture and hold the lightly defended airfield.

For six days MAG-24 aircraft poured fire down on the Japanese positions in support of US artillery. Once all three battalions were on the airfield, the wounded could be flown out and supplies brought in. A major supply depot was needed, which in turn required an amphibious landing at Macajalar Bay, and VMB-611 moved back to strike at the Del Monte area to support this venture.

Given a choice, Col Sarles would have stood his squadron down and ordered the overhaul of the PBJs, which had been flying hard for a month. But the ground situation took precedence, and on 2 May six aircraft were sent out in pairs at two-hourly intervals to bomb and strafe positions around the plateau. The third pair, piloted by Lts Wray E Bennett and Robert E Mason, dropped their bombs and split up. The latter pilot had, unwisely in the opinion of his crew chief, agreed to take two groundcrew passengers in the PBJ. Four hours had elapsed before Bennett's aircraft landed at Zamboanga. There was no sign of Mason.

What had transpired was the all too common, but often risky, 'one last pass' at the target. Dissatisfied with his previous rocket firing run, Mason went in again as the second PBJ turned for home. Bennett had noticed that both engines of Mason's PBJ were leaking oil. The scene was now set for a disaster. With two extra men on board, the PBJ would have had no chance of climbing out if an engine were hit. It was later confirmed that the notorious Japanese 37 mm flak had indeed shot the PBJ down, with the loss of all on board.

The following day Bennett went up to photograph Diklom airstrip near Del Monte, and to search for Mason's aircraft. As he approached the area, a Japanese Ki-21 'Sally' twin-engined bomber was spotted flying ahead of the PBJ. Bennett gave chase and the 'Sally' dove into a ravine, before climbing and dropping into another, with the PBJ in hot pursuit. Suddenly, the enemy pilot broke off and headed for Tagaloan airfield, probably low on fuel. He made a straight-in fast landing, with Bennett firing at the Ki-21 with his package guns. The opening rounds missed and Bennett hauled the PBJ round for a second shot, with bombardier S/Sgt John Stright using his nose gun. This time the bomber burst into flames.

This action alerted Sarles to the possibility that the enemy might be about to reinforce Tagaloan. Accordingly, on 4 May he sent seven PBJs out. They attacked in waves, the first pair dropping 1000-lb bombs from 8000 ft, before diving down to use rockets on a building east of the strip. Subjected to flak, these aircraft promptly strafed the offending gun emplacements. The second pair followed suit and demolished the airfield control tower with rockets, while the third PBJ duo dropped to 50 ft, intending to use delayed action bombs. But instead, with so much debris and smoke, they bombed one gun position and rocketed a second. PBJ number seven hardly got a look at the airfield through the smoke. Not to be outdone, its pilot bombed a couple of shacks, then came around to blow in the entrance to a storage cave and strafe an armoured car. It was a good piece of work, executed without casualties.

By 6 May Morozumi's position was growing more difficult by the hour. He could either fight it out against superior forces or retreat. He chose the latter course, aiming to cross Mindanao's eastern mountain range and reach the Agusan Valley. By so doing he ran headlong into the 108th Regimental Combat Team landing at Macajalar Bay. Above them, the Japanese troops would have seen the PBJs of VMB-611 flying 'support air observation' sorties. Each aircraft flew as part of a relay system and carried as an observer a 10th Corps officer who maintained contact with the ground forces and located targets for the Marine SBDs.

Two PBJs flew singly on these reconnaissance sorties, and by the afternoon of the landings the bombers found little to shoot at. The following day US troops came up against a Japanese defensive line south of Alae. The SBDs and F4Us were called in while the Mitchells continued to monitor the situation and pass reports. As a finale for VMB-611 in this sector of the Philippines fighting, four pairs of aircraft took off on 10 April to attack Panacan, Tupi, Tamugan and Galuman – all points along Morozumi's retreat route. It would be several weeks before those troops saw the blue medium bombers again.

During the fighting in the Bukidnon Valley VMB-611 had flown 173 sorties, dropped about 245 tons of bombs and fired 800 rockets, as well as expending thousands of rounds of ammunition. The unit had killed enemy troops, disrupted supply lines and destroyed artillery and stores for a cost of nine dead, nine wounded and four aircraft lost. Just 15 PBJs had been available during the entire period.

THE BATTLE OF DAVAO

Col Sarles remained VMB-611's driving force. Having experienced Japanese bombing during the early part of the war, he said;

'It is a tremendous pleasure to be carrying the big stick of air and surface power rather than to be on the other end. I have taken personal pleasure in taking night intruder missions over enemy positions, (and) two days ago I had a most interesting flight on which I landed at Del Monte, the formerly Jap-held airfield which we had bombed and otherwise attacked for over a month, and which our ground troops now hold.

'It was most instructive to see the actual results on the ground, and I was pleased that our estimate (of results) jibed so closely with the facts. Actually, I am immensely pleased that I have been so fortunate to remain in command of the squadron, and feel proud that it has come pretty near the high expectations I had for it.'

Although Gen Morozumi had been forced to retreat, he had not committed all his forces to a set-piece battle with the Americans which he had no hope of winning in the face of their overwhelming air superiority. Consequently, he sought to buy time and tie up as many US troops as possible to prevent them being used in the invasion of Japan. This intelligent reading of enemy intentions resulted in fairly light casualties on both sides, as the general was not about to sacrifice his men in a final, pointless banzai charge.

Gen Harada, on the other hand, was hungry for battle. He had been on Mindanao waiting for the Americans for some three years and intended to fight to the hilt of the Bushido code. He was better placed than Morozumi, having twice the number of men and considerably more equipment. Highway 1 from Parang ran straight into his fortified positions in the Davao Valley, making a bloody battle unavoidable. And Harada's defences were formidable. He made maximum use of terrain slashed by ravines and limestone gullies under a blanket of rain forest. Ground terraced for agriculture had been turned over to machine gun nests, and there were trench lines, concrete pillboxes, flak batteries and even six-inch naval guns in caves. Some 15,000 troops of the 100th Division manned these positions.

High ground known to the Americans as Hill 550 dominated the entire defensive line. In addition, Harada could count on a further 10,000 sailors and airmen of the 32nd Naval Base Force, as well as 7000 civilian auxiliaries. Into this cauldron would go Maj Gen Roscoe Woodruff's 24th Infantry Division, roughly equal in number to the enemy force. Woodruff counted on artillery and airpower to alter the odds in his favour and enable his infantry to take many of the positions with relative ease.

The battle began on 27 April when the 34th Regiment entered the town of Digos. Held up until the following day when the Japanese suddenly melted away, the Americans advanced to surprise the enemy in the act of blowing a bridge across the Talomo River. It was captured intact and held against several enemy assaults, enabling the Americans to advance. But it proved difficult to clear the trench lines even with tanks. Individual pillboxes had to be destroyed before the advance could proceed, and that was where MAGSZAM came in. It would take the Marine bombers about two weeks to clear these obstacles. They dropped 92 tons of bombs and 3.5 tons of napalm in 120 sorties to knock out 39 pillboxes.

Progress on the ground was steady, with the naval guns on the eastern end of Hill 550 being captured quickly. Davao City turned out to be a ghost town, all but abandoned by its inhabitants. Indeed, the enemy had driven out the Filipinos, and consequently the US felt free to bomb any area harbouring the Japanese. By 9 May the first phase of Woodruff's offensive was complete. VMB-611 had taken little part in the fighting, having ranged further afield in order to bomb and strafe behind the lines in the pass area. Between 16-20 May the PBJs flew 90+ sorties at Davao.

HUNTING PATROL BOATS

An unusual target presented itself to VMB-611's PBJs on 14 May. Accustomed to land targets, the crews were sent out to search the many inlets of the river running into Talomo Bay. It had been the scene of a daring attack by Japanese patrol boats on 10 May when a US transport bringing supplies to sustain the land battle was sunk by a spread of torpedoes. Air searches for the boats initially proved fruitless, but the PBJs had the fuel to make lengthy patrols, and at last their patience was rewarded. A cove at Pico Point was found to house not only a dock and buildings but torpedo loading hoists and a concrete pillbox. The PBJ crews decided to attack.

A low-level run with 250-lb bombs resulted in hits on all the structures, plus the demolition of a light framework which disguised five boats to look like a waterside house. On a third run the pilot strafed the boats and set one on fire. Another PBJ then took over and caused more damage, as did a third and a fourth. This combined attack left only one boat afloat and most of the dock facilities beyond repair.

Two days later the 34th Regiment was in a position to assault Hill 550 and thrust towards Mintal. Heavy air strikes preceded the advance, which found plenty of action. With tanks sent against the main Japanese defensive line, the battle raged for ten days. Again the PBJs played little part

A standard PBJ-1J is framed by the right wing of a second aircraft, the latter boasting the radome for the sea search radar. Transferring the radar to the wing required several long cable links which were prone to combat damage, and Marine groundcrews preferred to relocate the antenna to the nose (via Alan Carey)

in battlefield support, this task falling to the SBDs. Meanwhile, VMB-611's action against targets around Davao involved its share of excitement.

On 18 May Lt Cliff Schmillen, now promoted to aircraft captain, was en route to Davao when a Mayday message was received. A PT boat skipper was being attacked by six enemy torpedo boats and needed help fast. Schmillen raced to the spot, and dropping to 1500 ft, he saw the six-to-one contest. As the bomber came in, the Japanese boats scattered, and Schmillen carried out a methodical search for their hiding places. The PBJ's radioman, Sgt Frederick W Tymeson, stayed in touch with the beleaguered captain to receive directions, and for two hours the bomber and the PT boat worked together to find and destroy all six enemy vessels with guns, bombs and rockets. The action ended with the American PT boat cutting through the water at full throttle and the sailors waving wildly as the PBJ rocked its wings in salute.

For the bomber crews, such a sortie was marginally easier than working the ravines and gullies of the Kibawe Trail in support of the land battle. The Japanese proved to be tenacious and intelligent foes, retreating in good order and not indulging in sacrificial actions that would cause needless casualties.

Having little time to concentrate his guns on the PBJs, the enemy resorted to stretching cables across some of the routes used by low flying aircraft and firing at them with everything from small arms to 37 mm weapons. Friendly troops reported that the Japanese seemed more afraid of the PBJs than the SBDs, presumably because the bombers were so heavily armed. On 30 May Sarles ordered seven PBJs to sweep the Kibawa Trail in waves of three pairs of two, plus Maj Fagan. At that time Harada was retreating up the trail under cover of artillery at the base of Mount Apo (Mindanao's highest mountain), on the south side of the pass.

Lts Kronic and Horton piloted the first two PBJs, and they arrived over the pass at 0800 hrs to attack houses said to be occupied by the enemy. An hour later Sarles and Schmillen followed, the latter dropping nine bombs and firing eight rockets at troops in a ravine, while the colonel's PBJ veered off towards the base of Mount Apo to look for artillery.

He flew right over a group of camouflaged gun positions, glimpsed quickly as the PBJ passed. Turning, Sarles came back for a bomb run at tree-top level, and was almost immediately hit by 37 mm fire. The colonel tried to pull up, but the bomber's remaining engine could not generate sufficient power. One wing caught a tree and the PBJ smashed into the ground in a grinding, sliding crash for about 100 yards. Shortly afterwards, the bomb load exploded. Fagan was next into the target area. Informed that the colonel's PBJ was missing, he immediately began a search of the trail, but to no avail.

With Schmillen having returned to base, Lts Hoadley and Doit L Fish were the next to arrive. They were told about Sarles, and they joined in the search for the CO's downed PBJ. Hoadly flew up the Kibawe Trail while Fish turned south to follow the road – eight men were aboard the latter pilot's PBJ that day. The same number (including an extra passenger) had been aboard Sarles' PBJ, and of these, five, including the CO, were lost. Co-pilot Lt Albert E Fitch, tail gunner S/Sgt Arvid J Steiff and radioman Sgt Robert E Brow escaped the wreck, spread out and managed to make their way through enemy lines to safety. They were able to confirm that

Sarles had been last seen slumped in his seat, killed by enemy fire or from the injuries he had sustained in the crash.

The events of 30 May hit VMB-611 harder than anyone realised at the time. George Sarles had been both the head and heart of the squadron, and with his loss morale sagged. The unit remained in action, but its crews performed their missions without the same spirit or dedication that an exceptional leader can instill in those under his command.

By 1 July 1945, when the command of VMB-611 passed to Maj Robert R Davis, the squadron had completed a total of 437 sorties over Mindanao and the Sulus. Of these, 14 had been at night and nearly 600 tons of bombs had been dropped and 2400 rockets expended. These figures represented an average of 80,000 lbs of bombs and 160 rockets per aircraft. In April alone 244 sorties had been flown, with a further 193 being completed in May. Most significantly from the USMC planners' viewpoint, the same effort with single-engined bombers like the SBD would have involved 60 aircraft and 120 crewmen, compared with 15 PBJs and 90 crew.

BORNEO DIVERSION

During April 1945 the Australians had begun planning their campaign to capture the island of Borneo, south-west of Mindanao. A vital part of the Allied plan to invade Japan, Borneo was to have been, along with Okinawa and Mindanao, one of the main bases for the operation, scheduled for 1 November 1945. Borneo's oil production facilities had been destroyed in 1944, but the Japanese remained in possession of the island as VMB-611 arrived at Zamboanga in March. Moret Field was one of the nearest air bases to north Borneo, and it fell to VMB-611, as the only long-range bomber unit in MAGSZAM, to fly reconnaissance sorties before the Australians landed in June. Crews faced a round trip of 750 miles from Moret to Brunie, in Borneo, almost all over water. Flight time was up to six-and-a-half hours depending on the briefed time over target. The unit flew 21 sorties without any losses or mechanical problems – another tribute to the enduring skills of both flight and groundcrews.

During these Borneo missions the PBJ crews picked up much valuable intelligence about the enemy's strength. They observed shipping traffic, the inevitable flak batteries, which fired on the Marine bombers, a PoW camp and an airstrip. This seemed capable of handling fighters, the main airfield at Sandakan having evidently been rendered inoperable by Allied bombs. Troop movements were also noted although the size of the garrison seemed to be smaller than guerrilla reports had suggested.

On 9 June – the night before the Australians landed – Maj Davis, accompanied by Lts Pollan, Chelgen and Samuel Davis, flew out to Kudat, on the northern tip of

As part of the updating of the B-25, North American produced the definitive J-model, which became the PBJ-1J in Marine Corps service. The radar antenna was moved to the right wing, which some thought not as good a location as the nose, and some squadron aircraft were locally modified. A standard PBJ-1J is seen here, probably flying off the US coast on a training sortie (*Herb Lentsch*)

Borneo. Each PBJ, loaded with 500-lb bombs, patrolled the Brunie Bay area to keep the enemy awake.

When the Australians went ashore the following day, the PBJs flew over the landing area looking for Japanese patrol boats known to be operating in the vicinity. None was seen, and they proved elusive for the next two days. After that PBJ patrols ceased, and responsibility for providing air cover for the invasion passed to the Thirteenth US Army Air Force.

Early June was also a busy time for VMB-611, as it was required to fly escort missions with MAG-14 fighters based at Samar, north of Zamboanga. The F4Us had been ordered to Okinawa, and they needed navigators to help get them there safely. As VMB-611 was once again the only unit available, it was given the job. Most of its PBJs were involved in the movement, leaving just enough to handle the armed reconnaissance runs to Borneo. Other transfers were welcomed by 23 pilots and crews, who were to be rotated home after being replaced by new ones.

BACK TO THE JUNGLE

When the PBJs completed their runs to Okinawa on 15 June, the squadron resumed its support of 10th Corps by attacking two objectives. The first was the unit's old adversary Gen Morozumi and his forces, while the second was softening up defences at Sarangani Bay, where the US had planned to mount an amphibious landing on 12 July.

Morozumi was still operating in the Agusan Valley, where he had split his forces. The largest segment retreated east up a mountain trail behind Malabalay, while the smaller went southwards down the Kibawe Trail. Both groups were being pursued by separate American regiments, but the enemy had a knack of quickly building strong defensive positions in country that was ideal for the purpose. Morozumi's ambushes, some five miles from Malaybalay, continued to delay the advance – it took about a week to dislodge his troops. This period of stop-start combat continued through July, by which time the Japanese were all but exhausted. When they emerged on to the plain about Davao, Morozumi and his men looked up to see the PBJs of VMB-611 above them once again.

American troops on the Kibawe Trail had fared badly, difficult mountain terrain having been made worse by heavy rains. By mid-July the pursuit was abandoned, and the men returned to Kibawe town.

During June a concurrent fight to secure the foothills of the Davao Valley saw Marine SBDs doing their best to dislodge the enemy by bombing well dug-in caves and rain forest hideouts. Gen Harada moved into positions prepared many months before, his intention being to hold up the Americans for as long as possible – a number of flak sites formed part of the defences. That same month VMB-611 was asked to assist SBDs flying from airfields at Moret and Malabang, Fagan flying initially to Sarangani to act as air coordinator for an SBD strike. Orbiting at 9000 ft, he directed the dive-bombers, ignoring several burst of flak aimed at his PBJ.

Lts Chelgren and LeMasters joined in this attack by working from 0830 to 1000 hrs over a section of the beach, helping direct PT boats to their targets. In return, the boats directed the bombers to seek out enemy barges and landing craft which had brought in 2000 Japanese reinforcements. Chelgren found the barges and strafed them, before dropping eight 250-lb bombs on adjacent buildings and stacked oil drums.

The buildings went up in flames, but not the drums. Flying on to the nearby town of Buyuan, Chelgren saw trenches and dugouts being prepared alongside an abandoned airstrip north of Sarangani Bay.

Taking over from Chelgren at 1130 hrs, LeMasters made contact with the PT boats and proceeded to bomb and strafe the same area, this time hitting the oil drums. Continuing on to the trenches, LeMasters' co-pilot, Bob Jardes, hit a 12 ft by 210 ft concrete reinforced dugout dead centre with a 250-lb bomb. The crew finally shot up more oil drums, their bullets causing a spill but no fire. The attack continued the following day when Lt Stanley Kronick made contact with the PT boats and attacked the same dock area with bombs, followed by strafing. The aircraft of Lt William Pollan finished off the job, to the congratulations of the PT crews.

On 18 June Capt Chapman led a nine-aeroplane strike on the trench area. Ammunition dumps, five flak batteries and barracks buildings were now in evidence, and these were bombed and strafed with reportedly excellent results. More of the same followed on the 19th, Maj Davis leading a nine-PBJ formation carrying fragmentation bombs. He did the same on the 20th, a six-aeroplane flight breaking into two elements. The major's aircraft, and Lt Samuel Davis' PBJ 'MB-10', were about 60 ft apart as they ran in to the target. Flying as No 3, Lt Davis watched the major drop his bombs and followed suit at a height of about 200 ft. The major's ship turned right and passed below Lt Davis, who felt six light thumps under his aircraft.

As Davis watched the major's PBJ, the latter seemed to be under full control. Davis rolled his elevator tabs forward but felt no response until a crew member was called up to the cockpit so as to restore the PBJ's trim. Attempting to call up the major on both VHF and liaison radio sets, Davis found both to be inoperative. Circling the rendezvous point ten miles southwest of Clinan town, the lieutenant then reported seeing a column of heavy black smoke rising up to 600 ft, before heading home.

Upon returning to base, Davis and his crew counted four three-inch holes in the PBJ's wings, plus eight more of about six to eight inches in diameter in the fuselage. A large shrapnel fragment had come up through the forward part of the dorsal turret, chipping a gun breech and breaking the Plexiglas cover. It was subsequently determined that Davis' aircraft had been damaged by the detonation of the major's bombs, which had been impact-fused. Samuel Davis subsequently reported that as the second section came in at 1400 ft, following the direction of the first, flak was observed around the leading PBJs. As the section released its bombs, an aircraft was seen crossing the road south of Clinan town at about 100 ft. As they watched, a spurt of smoke came from the aircraft and it immediately burst into flames. This was confirmed to have been Maj Davis.

Other woes had befallen the lead section. Lt Robert Griffith, flying PBJ-1C 'MB-9', had been hit in one engine. The aircraft could not maintain altitude, and the pilot radioed that he had to ditch – at 1153 hrs the Mitchell hit the sea a mile offshore in Sarangani Bay. It took just four minutes to sink. Japanese flak had been deadly accurate that day, as aside from the two downed PBJs, Lt LeRoy Streit's bomber returned to base with two holes in it, and Lt Albers (secondary lead) counted three hits.

Reports further indicated that the first section, with Davis leading, had dropped fragmentation bombs from very low altitude, and that instantaneous fusing had caused damage to the CO's aircraft, as well as that of Lt Griffith, although the heavy flak barrage left this in doubt. Four of Griffith's crew survived the ditching, although two were seriously wounded and three were killed. Maj Davis had continued from the initial bomb run to strafe enemy troops seen near Clinan, and was hit by flak while doing so. One engine was knocked out and the hydraulic system was set on fire, but contrary to Lt Davis' report, the major had been able to crash land in a field, despite his hands and face being badly burned.

The impact had knocked co-pilot Lt Coons unconscious in his seat and severely injured navigator-bombardier M/Tech/Sgt Ivan Fritz's back when he slammed against the cockpit bulkhead. Also badly banged about were S/Sgt Carveth, who had difficulty moving, and Cpl Bombard and S/Sgt Flynn, who were both hurt, but mobile. Davis and Fritz escaped through the top hatch, thinking Coons would follow. Flynn helped pull the co-pilot out, despite licking flames. Other crewmen helped each other, but knowing the rising column of smoke from the crashed PBJ would soon attract the Japanese, Coons took charge.

After a hazardous and uncomfortable walk, the crew reached a Filipino beach house. A hand mirror and some marker dye spread on the water attracted the attention of a flight of SBDs. They radioed a Playmate PBY, which landed in the bay. Davis, Coons and Fritz were flown to Leyte, while the others were admitted to the Army hospital at Zamboanga.

REPLACEMENTS

With replacements arriving from the US, original PBJ crews were rotated home. All, that is, except experienced navigator-bombardiers, whose expertise was too valuable to lose. Consequently, these men anticipated a long haul right through to the invasion of Japan. In the way of military men, they did not rate their chances of surviving that operation too highly. Then, of course, nobody knew anything about the atomic bomb, so they anticipated that the prevailing 27 per cent casualty rate would rise when the massive amphibious operation got underway. This was a difficult period for long-serving squadron members. Those veterans of earlier operations now faced a different set-up with pilots who were strangers to them, and a new CO – Maj David Horne officially took over on 20 June.

VMB-611 flew 98 sorties in June 1945, with about half of these being reconnaissance missions and the rest almost equally split between night bombing and formation daylight attacks. Large formation strikes were flown at the end of the month for the benefit of new crews, the latter being slowly introduced to combat, having not been deemed ready to work independently. That the war was winding down was reflected in July's activities, when most missions were flown at night. The PBJs were dropping leaflets calling on the enemy to surrender.

The squadron continued to receive PBJ-1C/Ds as replacements, and they were deployed in much the same way as before. Typically, six-aeroplane, low level strikes were made on the Kibawe Trail area, where the retreating Japanese remained active.

The PBJs also flew weather flights on a daily basis – a service vital to mission planning. In July, missions were interspersed with transport and ferry flights, the routine air testing of replacement parts following repairs and a steady flow of new personnel. But it was clear to all concerned that the Americans on Mindanao had reached the mopping-up stage of the occupation, with the Japanese steadily giving ground on all the remaining Philippine battle fronts.

JAPANESE ASSISTANCE

An incident that has passed into Marine close air support lore involved a mission flown by 2Lt Minoru Wada. The opportunity of carrying a Japanese soldier in the waist of a PBJ as he guided American bombers and fighters in to obliterate his own headquarters seemed a US public relations dream. Wada duly climbed aboard one of VMB-611's PBJ-1Js on 10 August, and he did indeed call out coordinates to the formation, which probably bombed accurately enough to kill Gen Harada, who still led the Imperial Japanese Army's tough 100th Division. His HQ was a primary target for that particular PBJ mission to the Upian area of Mindanao.

Wada had been born in the US and was a student in Japan when war was declared. Trapped by circumstances, he had no choice but to accept the Army draft. However, you don't (as the saying goes) have to like it, and Wada surrendered to US forces in the Philippines and agreed to help the Marines pin-point Harada's position. He was photographed at the briefing with Marine crews and several times throughout the mission by Lt David Duncan.

The Americans failed fully to appreciate Wada's action, assuming either that he had harboured burning hatred for his CO, or that he had been punished for some transgression. Understandably, Wada appeared to be experiencing mixed emotions as the Marines' bombs fell. The bombing was quite accurate, and the PBJs then went down to rocket and strafe the area, being well covered by the F4Us of VMF-115.

During April and May 1945, VMB-611's crews flew 437 sorties for a 27 per cent casualty rate. Losses including George Sarles, who had done so much to put his unit and its aircraft on the map. Maj Gen Ralph Mitchell, commander of the 1st MAW, later said of VMB-611's part in the Philippines campaign, 'I am delighted with the work of this squadron. It very definitely has delivered a Sunday punch'.

When the rumours of a US 'super bomb' capable of wiping out a whole city were found to be fact and not unreliable scuttlebutt, the men of VMB-611 began to think that at last the war would end without the feared invasion of Japan. They knew for sure when Adm Chester Nimitz came on the radio on 14 August and said, 'This is a peace warning'.

For some members of VMB-611, though, the long-anticipated home-coming would have to await events unfolding in China.

In the aftermath of the Russian invasion of Manchuria, the rise of

One of the more bizarre incidents of the war was the voluntary offer by Japanese army officer 2Lt Minoru Wada to guide VMB-611 PBJs straight to his unit's headquarters on Mindanao, in the Philippines, shortly before Japan surrendered. Approaching the area, this mixed formation of PBJ-1D/Js prepares for bombs away, well covered by their VMF-115 F4U Corsair escort (*Agencies/IWM*)

1Lt Wada coordinates the 10 August attack, acting as formation 'lead bombardier'. Using a microphone in the waist position of a PBJ, he passes radio messages to the pilot, and watches, grim-faced, as the bombs go down. The Marine flyers were at a loss to know why he had volunteered to help them in this way (*USMC*)

the communist guerrilla movement and the uncertain position of the US-backed nationalist regime, Washington sought to impose a Western buffer against the Russians overstaying their welcome, and to oversee proper disarmament of the Japanese. To assist Chiang Kai-shek oust the communists, the US Navy shipped troops back to Japan, and the 6th Marine Division was despatched to undertake a policing role. The ground troops were followed by the 1st Marine Air Wing, with MAG-32 and -25 flying to Tsingtao, MAG-12 to Tientsin and MAG-24 to Peking.

VMB-611's primary role during this strange period was to fly navigation escort to 1st MAW's SBDs and F4Us across the China Sea from Okinawa. The PBJ squadron had flown to Okinawa from Mindanao after VJ-Day, and by early October it was ready for the China deployment. Since the assignment was to be a temporary one, most of the groundcrews were left behind at Zamboanga. Those who did go were charged with ensuring proper maintenance and refuelling of the aircraft between flights.

On 21 October the PBJs took off for Okinawa. All the pilots and most of the crews were post-war replacements, the long-suffering navigator-bombardiers being virtually the only combat veterans left. The trip took two days, with a stop-over at Laong, in northern Luzon. At Chima Field, Okinawa, the fighters and dive-bombers of the 1st Wing were lined up like chicks waiting for their mother hens. Over several days each PBJ left with a clutch of fighters and dive-bombers, each group making its way individually westwards across the China Sea. Landing with their charges at Shanghai, the PBJ crews found they had time on their hands. In view of the local attractions (invariably female), many wanted to stay indefinitely. Numerous technical malfunctions were found to extend this period of enjoyable R&R for as long as possible.

Inevitably, it all came to an end, and the PBJs made their way to Tientsin and then Peking. VMB-611 finally left China on 30 October to return to the Philippines. All that remained was to service the PBJs for the flight to Pelelieu, the first stop on the homeward trip across the Pacific. Most of the unit's effects were destroyed, but the gear that was to return was loaded aboard the USS *Gallatin*, which sailed on 8 November – five days before the PBJs had taken off from Zamboanga for the last time.

With stops at Guam, Wake Island and Midway, the PBJs finally landed at Ewa Marine Air Base, at Pearl Harbor, on 8 November, where the aircraft were turned over to guards who had orders to dump them into the ocean. That was a particularly hard decision for some of the veterans to understand, but on reflection they came to terms with the fact that the war was finally over.

SAIPAN AND IWO

Compared to the dangerous routine of blockading Rabaul and other bypassed Japanese bases, not to mention the struggle to secure the Philippines, VMB-612's autumn 1944 movement orders appeared to offer a change of scene. There was also the promise of a kind of action different to that being experienced by other Marine Mitchell squadrons, although such comparisons were not possible as the unit prepared to ship out to the Central Pacific for its first active duty station. VMB-612's PBJs soon reached Saipan, the Marianas island which assumed a vital role in the heavy bomber campaign against the Japanese empire.

Saipan had supposedly been secured the previous June, but there were still Japanese there who had not yet heard of the island's change of control. These diehards were to give VMB-612 some headaches in subsequent weeks, but they were not the only source of discomfort. Arriving on 28 October 1944, VMB-612's 16 PBJ-1Ds were assigned to Kagman Point airfield, but ground personnel had first been obliged to virtually build the strip themselves in order to make it habitable. Therefore, it was not until 13 November that the squadron was able to fly its first mission – a search for shipping that took Col Cram and his five-man crew out to

VMB-612's pilots pose for an official photograph shortly after the squadron's arrival on Saipan, in the Marianas, in late October 1944. The 'hose nose' PBJ appears to be watching over its human assets (*via Thomas Honeycutt*)

the Bonin and Kazan Islands area. Cram returned claiming to have sunk a submarine and a 'patrol boat'.

The Marine flyers soon received the inevitable welcome to Saipan from 'Tokyo Rose', who made it clear to the unit that someone was watching their bombers very closely when she referred to the '20 mm cannon' in the tail position of the PBJ. This error was apparently caused by the fitment of blast tubes over the barrel of the single machine gun, which gave the weapon a fatter silhouette.

Lt Samuel C Balthrop's PBJ BuNo 35201 became VMB-612's first combat loss when he ditched on the night of 16/17 November 1944. A photographer riding in Lt James Powell's PBJ took this shot of the downed aeroplane. Four crewmen survived this incident, only to be killed on 20 April 1945 when Lt Balthrop crashed in fog whilst attempting to land on Iwo Jima (*via Thomas Honeycutt*)

DITCHING FEARS

The first days of November proved uneventful despite several operational sorties. Japanese shipping was becoming scarce, but on the night of the 16/17th Cram found and attacked three medium sized freighters and a fourth vessel. The CO reported three hits, but in the absence of strike photos, the damage remained undetermined. That same night 2Lt Samuel C Balthrop's PBJ-1D (BuNo 35201) ran out of fuel. Taking to their dinghy, four of the crew were recovered by a destroyer after eight hours in the water. However, the loss of two men in the incident raised questions about the correct procedure for ditching a PBJ.

At that time the squadron had little idea about just how far it could fly with its PBJs in military fit – full fuel, six-man crew and weapons – so it consequently conducted assessment flights to determine endurance, and thus avoid further instances of 'running out of gas'. But data gained in this way was always dependent on powerplant condition, and could be upset by an engine change. As PBJ veteran Roger Sanders said, 'I'd much rather fly an engine which had been running for 500 hours than a brand-new one. You knew what the old one was going to do'.

In a ditching, it seemed that most occupants suffered some degree of injury when an aircraft hit the sea, and there was little that could be done beyond stressing the importance of being firmly strapped in. But there was some psychological barrier to this when escape was required in a matter of seconds. Rescue services provided by submarines, ships and PBY Dumbos were in place, and they were generally efficient, but everything depended on how soon the downed aircraft could be located. Squadron PBJs always conducted immediate searches for any downed crew, and these were not abandoned until all hope of recovery had to be given up.

Just how easily a crew could be lost was demonstrated on 26 November during a five-aeroplane strike on Dunker's Derby, the blind bombing area assigned to the squadron. 1Lt Edward Madvay and his crew in PBJ-1D BuNo 35156 ditched in a known position, but daylight searches by VMB-612 aircraft over the next few days brought home the appalling fact that a bomber the size of a PBJ, and its entire six-man crew could apparently vanish into thin air.

On the 28th VMB-612 attacked the island of Haha Jima. No shipping was found, but a PBJ crew fired rockets at what appeared to be an ammunition dump on the island. The waters of Dunker's Derby also proved unproductive in terms of shipping, and another PBJ fired rockets into the town of Okimura. Columns of smoke were seen.

Bright moonlit nights were generally bad for PBJ operations. So too were harbours, as they were usually defended by heavy calibre weapons. November concluded with the loss of yet another PBJ in unknown circumstances when 1Lt Cleo J Falgout failed to make any position reports after taking off in PBJ-1D BuNo 35149 on the 30th. None of the six-man crew was seen again, and all were declared missing in action. It was suggested that Falgout, being a little gung ho, might have charged into Chichi Jima harbour intent on sinking as many ships as he could all at once.

During its first month on Saipan VMB-612 recorded 159 individual flights for the loss of three PBJs and 13 crew members. Throughout November the work of stripping equipment out of the aircraft had continued unabated. This included modifying the upper bomb-bay fuel tanks to feed through selector valves in the navigator's compartment, which in turn allowed operation independent of the lower tank. A CO_2 purging system was also installed for the lower tank.

Tests, however, proved that even when purged, the tanks retained inflammable fuel vapour. New self-sealing tanks were quickly ordered from the US, but crews were warned not to go charging into well defended areas where a PBJ was likely to take hits from flak.

Most of 'Cram's Rams'' PBJs are visible in this view of the squadron area on Saipan, which was shared with P-47s and P-38 of the Seventh Air Force's 318th FG. The Marine area was well served with access roads, the inevitable tents and a single hanger for undercover maintenance (*via Thomas Honeycutt*)

Stripping most of the PBJs' armament led to redundancies among VMB-612's gunners. Some re-mustered as navigator-bombardiers, attending ground schools established on Saipan before rejoining crews in time to see combat. Such training allowed them to make a more positive contribution, in their view, than building Quonset huts, which was all that was otherwise offered to those whose crew position had disappeared.

RECORD-SETTING

That ill luck tends to come in cycles was evident for VMB-612 after its November losses. Thereafter, the squadron settled into a pattern of missions which were generally conducted in relative safety for some time. Experience told pilots and groundcrews that every PBJ possessed its own characteristics in terms of fuel consumption, handling, control responses and so forth. Combining these variables with human nature could create complex problems which took time to resolve. There were other challenges posed by operational flying.

On 13 December Jack Cram took off for a strike on Chichi Jima. At some point in the flight, probably during a run on Kito Two, the starboard engine went out. Opinion varied as to why – one man believed the IFF aerial had broken off and been sucked into the engine, while another suggested the engine simply 'blew a stack'. Whatever the cause the result was that the engine had to be shut down and the propeller feathered. This left Cram with the prospect of a 650-mile return flight on one engine. When his aircraft appeared over the runway threshold, the squadron claimed he had set the record for the longest-ever over water flight on one engine. Cram made his usual smooth landing, but the other engine died as he turned off the runway. It was completely out of fuel.

With enemy shipping scarce, the PBJs often flew patrols which did not seem to achieve much. But this was not a view shared by the B-29 crews, who were grateful for the escort service provided by the Marines as they led them home from their raids on Japan, transmitting position reports along the way. Shipping attacks also remained problematical in terms of positive identification. There were so many US vessels in the PBJs' patrol areas that mistakes were waiting to happen. Fortunately, the Marine fliers generally managed to avoid errors of this kind, but frustration commonly accompanied post-action reports when results could not be verified.

Only five attacks were recorded in December, the problem with the bomb-bay fuel tanks persisting. As they could not be made completely safe, crews were understandably wary. Yet the folks back home would hardly have guessed at any such drawbacks. Squadron personnel wrote stories about VMB-612, playing up its role in the subjugation of Japan, and war correspondents made their way to Saipan to see 'Cram's Rams' in action. Well-known 'names' such as Ernie Pyle, Don Pryor of CBS and Vern Hangland of Associated Press added fuel to the fire that the squadron was stoking up in the Pacific.

SAIPAN – JANUARY 1945

On 2 January 1945 a returning PBJ was followed to its base by a Japanese aircraft, later identified in a victory claim as a Nakajima C6N 'Myrt'. Condor base (Saipan) ordered the Mitchell to circle and the enemy following suit until a 318th FG P-38 appeared on the scene and promptly shot it down in flames – an event witnessed by the PBJ crew. At that time life for the Marine medium crews on Saipan was punctuated by alerts of enemy air activity and operations which frequently failed to materialise. Having hunkered down to await falling bombs, none came. Then the crews would fly a mission, find no contacts and return. Alternatively, as on the 5th, the PBJs could find their patrols overlapping into an 'air search zone', which meant that any ships detected were not to be attacked as they could not be identified beyond doubt as Japanese.

PBJ crews were usually able to contact friendly surface forces to avoid potentially hazardous incidents on their search missions. These sorties could be frustrating in other ways, as was the case on 11 January when an aircraft attempted a run on a 30-ft sailing boat, but the target was so small that it did not provide an adequate radar blip for the crew. And then the weather intervened. Three days later a six-ship Japanese convoy was attacked, but poor visibility prevented any results from being observed.

On several occasions the weather closed in before the results of strikes could be verified, although crews saw flashes of flame which convinced them that ships had at least been damaged. Follow-up sorties to the same area the next night sometimes brought verification of a crippled vessel, although positive sightings could still be hampered by bad weather.

Compared with the target famine of the first two weeks of January, the 19th brought some more positive action. Two aircraft were involved in attacks on separate vessels, one of which was hit twice, with resultant fire being seen. The other PBJ, 'Fox-Baker', fought back. While evading the flak, the crew released two Mk 46 photoflash bombs to blind the enemy

This aerial view of VMB-612's dispersal area on Saipan reveals sea blue PBJ-1Ds scattered around a short taxiway at the northern end of Kagman Field's runway in mid-January 1945 (*via Thomas Honeycutt*)

gunners. Smoke was observed as the aircraft left the scene. These bombs, intended to illuminate targets for post-strike photography, were found to be effective in ruining enemy gunners' night vision, and they were regularly used for this purpose on combat missions. This went some way to explaining why the nocturnal anti-shipping record of the PBJ squadrons was rarely captured on film.

More action took place on the night of 21/22 January when a single PBJ detected two enemy vessels. One was attacked and five hits were observed by the crew of the aircraft, which then left the scene for some 15 minutes before returning. Only one vessel was visible, which indicated that the one hit earlier had gone down. A second PBJ operating that night broke off its attack when intercepted by a Japanese single-engined aircraft. Having failed to shake off the fighter, the crew made a second run on the vessel with the enemy aircraft latched onto the tail of their PBJ. The Marines bombed and five hits were observed, after which a series of diving turns and fire-walling the throttles saw the pilot lose his pursuer.

This kind of operational activity set a pattern for succeeding weeks – one or two PBJs scoring hits on various classes of enemy merchant vessel, but with few confirmed sinkings. Rockets as well as bombs were used during this period, the former being deployed on 29/30 January when four ships were hit. Two destroyers were struck by two rockets fired from a single PBJ-1D, with a third claimed as damaged by four rockets. A 'Fox Tare Charlie' (the numerous smaller Japanese vessels – fishing boats, cutters and other inshore craft – encountered by US aircraft were identified by a series of easy reference code names based on tonnage, design and armament) was also hit and appeared to be in distress as the PBJ left the scene.

During January 1945 VMB-612 had maintained a strength of 13 PBJ-1Ds without loss, with an average of eight being serviceable on a daily basis. Eight individual flights had resulted in action for the participating crews, and the unit had completed 100 combat sorties during the month.

As with other PBJ units, VMB-612 had trained on the PBJ-1C/D and had flown the early model B-25 equivalents since entering combat. North American Aviation had, in the meantime, produced the refined PBJ-1J, and initial examples of this final wartime model were en route to the Pacific to reach the squadron in March 1945. In common with other Mitchell units, VMB-612 supplanted its older aircraft with J-models, rather than replacing them. Indeed, many of its PBJ-1C/D soldiered on until VJ-Day. Between missions training continued, with squadron navigator-bombardiers being given individual instruction in radar calibration.

SAIPAN – FEBRUARY

The second month of 1945 proved a busy one for VMB-612, although there was still frustration at the failure to find targets. An experimental search procedure coordinated with Navy PB4Y Liberator

VMB-612's S/Sgt George E Lenhart uses a stray current tester (Ohm meter) prior to attaching rocket 'pig tails' to the aircraft's electrical firing system. This check was performed at the end of the runway just before take off to ensure that no stray current was detected – the latter could cause the rockets to fire off prematurely (*via Alan Carey*)

patrol bombers was initiated on 31 January, and this lasted three days. The Navy aircraft left Tinian at 0330 hrs each morning and two PBJs followed at 0530 hrs. Listening in to frequencies used by the Navy crews searching for shipping yielded no contacts for the Marines, who also listened out in vain. On the 7th a PBJ did make an attack on a large enemy vessel, the pilot firing all eight of his rockets – a large explosion was observed. Another PBJ expended two rockets on a smaller vessel, with unobserved results, while a third vessel received a full salvo of rockets, but bad weather prevented positive results from being observed.

An incident on 8 February highlighted the importance of installing AN/APS-3 tail warning radar in the squadron's PBJs. An unknown enemy aircraft was detected by one of only two PBJs in the unit to then be equipped with the radar, and the pilot soon lost his unseen assailant by executing a series of sharp turns down to 200 ft. Only five sets had been made available to the squadron, and in the wake of this sortie modification work was hastily put in hand to allow the equipment to be easily moved from aircraft to aircraft, as required.

The unit experienced its fourth combat loss on the 11th when 1Lt Clifford L James and his crew went missing. Again, there were theories that another gung-ho pilot had gone after a risky plum target. This time the word was that James had headed for Iwo, and the large number of Japanese aircraft reported on a strip there. James and his crew had been part of a six-aeroplane strike on the Bonin and Volcano Islands area which had, on the 10th, been the subject of an order to increase the number of aircraft on searches, thereby dissuading the enemy from trying to reinforce Iwo.

Participating crews found a medium-sized tanker, which was set ablaze after eight rockets were fired at it. A second PBJ encountered a target that could not be identified, and was therefore not attacked, whilst a third PBJ went after a large freighter. All eight rockets were seen to strike home, followed by a huge explosion. A fourth Mitchell was deterred from attacking anything when it was chased by a nightfighter – evading it used up too much fuel, and the pilot was obliged to return to base.

As the fight for Iwo Jima raged, staff deliberations decreed that the surrounding ocean areas should be made 'off limits' to friendly aircraft.

Running up its engines prior to departing on a sortie from Iwo Jima, this VMB-612 PBJ-1D has its bomb-bay doors open to purge the aircraft of any heat or fumes that may have built up inside the bomber prior to take off. Iwo Jima experiences extremely high temperatures for much of the year (*North American Aviation*)

The fear of mistaken identity by aircrew, ground troops and sailors was just too great until the island was secured. In the waning days of its Saipan sojourn, VMB-612 began receiving PBJ-1Js. During the first week of March BuNo 35234 was recorded as the first arrival, followed by 35239 and 35242. Accompanying each aircraft were two officers and three enlisted men who would join the squadron. A PBJ-1J required about one week to tailor it to VMB-612's requirements, as every example was unpainted and fully armed with turrets, package guns and so on.

On 7 March the squadron began search missions to the Marcus Islands area. Crews were ordered only to search and report anything of interes, as their patrol area was a designated 'air/surface zone'. On the 11th VMB-612 was allocated a blind bombing area around Marcus where it could expend rockets at targets of opportunity. None was found to justify the 1450-mile round trip, however. Then, on 13 March, the number of aircraft on search missions was reduced from three to two, with three on standby. Flights were also limited to three nights a week instead of seven

FORWARD TO IWO

Iwo Jima, which was virtually secured by the Americans by March 1945, was to be VMB-612's new home. On 6 April Cram led the squadron from the Marianas to the pork chop-shaped island that lay roughly halfway between Saipan and Japan. Each PBJ was lightened to increase its range, and any equipment regarded as non-essential was removed. PBJ-1D and Js with very light defensive armament would be operated from then on.

Flight duration between the islands was up to 12 hours, and crews were warned that the distance was equal to the extreme range of the PBJ – any aircraft disabled by fire or other causes would be unlikely to make it. This lighter configuration proved quite acceptable to the flight crews, and few PBJ-1Ds were restored to their former heavily-armed state upon their arrival on Iwo. There was little to fear from enemy interceptions, and the weight of additional guns and ammunition only added to the risk of aircraft loss in the event of damage. Only the single 'fifty' in the extreme tail was retained to deter would-be interceptors. In place of the guns the PBJs carried eight under-wing HVARs, plus bombs. It was a weapons load reckoned to be more than adequate to deal with any Japanese targets that the crews might find.

Aircrews and aircraft made the transfer from Saipan in several stages. VMB-612's new home was to be Iwo's Airfield Number One, located on the southern end of the island in the shadow of Mount Suribachi, the inactive volcano that hit the headlines when the 3rd and 5th Marines stormed it and raised the US flag. The unit was also notified that as of the 7th it would be under VII Fighter Command tactical control.

Flight operations began on the 9th, and at first the PBJs were restricted to a patrol area within a 40-mile radius of the island. The sectors were soon extended, and on the 10th Maj Fox flew VMB-612's first strike on Japan itself. The only

PBJ-1D 'White 10' of 'Cram's Rams', seen flying off Iwo Jima, displays the not untypical waist windows below the dorsal turret, the 'hose nose' radome and the gun gas dispenser under the forward fuselage (*Scarborough*)

target turned out to be a small vessel off the city of Kobe. Fox reported hitting it, but could not file a damage report.

Anti-submarine patrols were flown during this period, the routine being that three PBJs operated each night – one patrolled Hachijo Jima, one worked further north up to Tokyo Bay and the third undertook an ASW patrol. The crews relished these short flights, having spent hours in the air when flying out of Saipan. Shorter journey times to and from the target areas also meant that crews could remain on patrol, looking for enemy vessels, for longer. Even so, sightings did not increase significantly.

When ships were sighted, the crews had the time – if they had the inclination – to expend all munitions, fly home, rearm and go back for another try. This happened to Lt Francis H Russell's crew on the night of 13/14 April, when the PBJ attacked a merchant ship with all eight rockets and then flew back to Iwo to hastily reload. Heading back out with another war load, the crew was forced to abort its mission when a radio altimeter failed.

On reflection, the decision was a relief for at least one member of the crew, Sgt Ivan M Roberts. It was his 13th mission on Friday the 13th. 'When we were between Chichi and Haha Jima, in the northern Bonins, we ran into two Jap ships that we just couldn't pass up', he said. Lt Russell decided to use all the precious rockets on the freighter, despite a storm reducing visibility almost to zero. Roberts takes up the story;

'The weather was so bad up there that we had to make several runs on the ship to check course and position before firing. We came in so fast on our run that I guess the Japs never knew what hit them. But we could see all the shots hit home as we circled to return to Iwo for more rockets.'

Roberts reckoned that the severely damaged ship, which had been deserted by its escort vessel, would have made an easy kill on their second attack.

Night flying was suspended on 15 April, but on the 16th five PBJs were despatched on a daylight rocket strike to Kushira airfield, Kyushu. P-51s of the 531st FS picked up the Marine mediums at around 0900 hrs and escorted them to the home islands. The PBJ crews duly plastered the runway intersection at Kushira, together with repair shops and hangars at Kanoya East airfield. There had been no aircraft losses or crew casualties

An excellent portrait of VMB-612's PBJ-1D 'White 9' off Iwo Jima (or Saipan), 'slow timing' a new engine in 1945. The squadron retained the older D-models until the end of the war, although PBJ-1Js trickled in both before and after the Japanese surrender. The overpainted windows of the bombardier's station are clearly visible

A PBJ-1H banks away from the camera during a test firing flight of the aircraft's 75 mm cannon. Always impressive when the button was pressed, the big gun needed the right target, but few presented themselves to VMB-613 in 1945, the only Marine Corps unit fully equipped with the sub-type for Pacific operations (*North American Aviation*)

before the PBJs turned for home, but then a drama unfolded for Lt Daniel R Kingsley and his crew.

Flying BuNo 35161 'White MB-6', the crew was attacked at 1522 hrs by five F4U Corsairs en route to Okinawa – the designated diversionary area. For the duration of the short running fight, Kingsley frantically waggled his wings so as to bring the US national insignia to the attention of the over-eager fighter pilots. Not to be denied the kill, the F4Us also ignored the PBJ's IFF and frantic radio calls on VHF 'C' channel, 'hosing' the bomber enough for its pilot to have to perform a controlled ditching – by which point two crewmen had already baled out. In a fine feat of airmanship Kingsley brought the aircraft to rest, and it floated long enough for the four remaining crew members to vacate their positions. Of these, Kingsley and two other men were rescued by a PBM Mariner, but the remaining two who had taken to their parachutes were not found.

It appears from official records that several units may have been responsible for this case of mistaken identity. The pilots were probably well aware of rumours that the enemy was using captured US aircraft against them, and had therefore taken no chances by assuming an unfamiliar type to be hostile. The 16th was a day of intense aerial combat, with US Navy and Marine F4Us working hard to keep *kamikazes* from getting through to their two primary targets – the carriers and radar picket ships. It is also

possible that Corsairs of the British Pacific Fleet were in the area, but although several twin-engined Japanese bombers (for which the PBJ must have been mistaken) were shot down, the times seem at variance with the report detailing the PBJ loss. No Navy or Marine F4Us apparently claimed a twin-engined type at the time the PBJ ditched.

VMB-612 enjoyed a brief interlude after this action when the PBJ-1Hs of VMB-613 appeared in-theatre on a temporary duty assignment.

If there was one major problem with the otherwise convenient location of Iwo Jima it was fog. The island could become socked in very rapidly. much to the despair of weary B-29 crews seeking refuge. Despite the presence of a GCA station on the island, the PBJs also experienced problems.

On 20 April three PBJs returning from a mission found Iwo completely covered by fog. Ground control attempted to guide them in, but one of VMB-612's PBJ-1Js crashed short of the runway, killing Lt Balthrop and his crew. Two other PBJ-1Ds (BuNos 35148 and 35189) were forced to ditch without injury. The squadron had lost three aircraft to cancel out the recent arrival of three replacement PBJ-1Js, thus reducing its in ventory to 15 aircraft. VMB-612 also a small number of PBJs still based

Rocket-armed 'White 5' of VMB-612 taxies out on Iwo Jima, again with the precautionary open bomb-bay doors. Despite numerous contacts with enemy shipping, the number of definite sinkings achieved by the unit remained hard to determine due to a variety of factors (*North American Aviation*)

This close up view of VMB-612's 'White 9' reveals its unusual enclosed waist gun window. Pilot Roger M Sanders is standing to the left in the back row, with co-pilot Clyde I 'Cast Iron' Henderson and navigator-bombardier George H Moffett alongside him (*via Thomas Honeycutt*)

on Saipan, this machines having been left behind until Kagman Point airfield (formerly East Field) was deemed ready to accommodate them.

In addition to the sudden, but occasional, appearance of suicidal Japanese troops and snipers within the VMB-612 compound, there were nightly air raids by enemy bombers flying from bases on nearby mainland Japan. On Iwo itself, the enemy was usually wiped out before doing much damage. Mass gatherings of US personnel at movies, the mess hall or beach parties were considered targets by these fanatics, who invariably made the supreme sacrifice when conducting their suicidal attacks.

On 24 April VMB-612 was directed to begin harassing operations in the Bonin Islands area. Shipping was given first priority, but if none was found rockets were to be expended on land targets. Several late April missions were flown, but few targets of any note were found. New, more powerful aerial rockets were shipped to Iwo for VMB-612 at this time, although relatively few were to find their way under the wings of the PBJs. Utilising a five-inch explosive head on a Mk 6 body, the new rockets had a greater velocity than the previous 3¼-inch type.

Supplies of the new weapon effectively stopped on 25 April when a fire broke out in an Army ammunition dump and destroyed about 1300 rocket motors and 2300 bodies!

MAY 1945

A mission on 2 May resulted in unusual action for 1Lt John F Jarrell and his crew when they were shot at with great accuracy by shore-based flak batteries whilst attacking a large tanker. Flying PBJ-1D BuNo 35156, Jarrell was on a search mission off Hagahi Minato when he spotted the vessel at anchored. Diving at the ship from a height of 3000 ft, intending to glide bomb it, Jarrell's PBJ had its port vertical stabiliser and part of its tailplane shot away by 75 mm and 90 mm flak rounds. At about 700 ft the pilot managed to veer away from the fiercest concentration of fire and engage the autopilot, thus allowing both Jarrell and his co-pilot to hold onto the controls and stop the aircraft from plunging into the sea. They pointed the bomber back towards Iwo Jima.

Jarrell called Agate base (Iwo) and all ships in the area to watch for the crew's parachutes. Despite this precaution, only two men survived the jump from the stricken PBJ, Jarrell perishing when he remained with the aircraft – co-pilot 1Lt Harold Darling and radioman S/Sgt Leon Sutton were rescued. These losses once more highlighted the odds against all occupants of a PBJ baling out safely.

Following the departure of VMB-613's PBJ-1Hs from Iwo, 24 May recorded some anti-shipping activity for VMB-612. A single PBJ left a 75-ft patrol boat in flames, before turning its attention to a 400-ft 'Sugar Able Uncle'. This was also sunk in an action which aroused the interest of two enemy nightfighters – both were successfully evaded, however. A second PBJ out hunting that night attacked a 'Sugar Dog' but missed it.

Several more largely unproductive sorties were flown prior to the arrival of an evaluation unit on the island on 28 May. This five-man team, equipped with cameras and other equipment, was there to initiate VMB-612's personnel into the mighty 11.75-in 'Tiny Tim' rocket. Jack Cram returned to the unit on 29 May, and two days later word was received by the unit to pack up and leave Iwo Jima for Okinawa.

ROCKET ISLAND

Generally speaking, the United States Navy's aerial ordnance in World War 2 was based on a series of standard weapons ranging from the 0.50-cal machine gun through a variety of bombs and depth charges to the high velocity rocket. It was left to the versatile B-25/PBJ to deploy more exotic weaponry in combat, including the 75 mm cannon, the Mk 41 glide torpedo (in Army service) and, finally, the 'Tiny Tim' air-to-surface rocket with the Marines.

This 11.75-in weapon was a standard 500-lb Semi-Armour Piercing M 58A1 bomb filled with TNT and attached to a steel tube, the latter being fitted with a motor and cruciform fins. It had an overall length of 123 inches and weighed 600 lbs. The weapon was briefly deployed in combat by F4Us but then abandoned for use by Navy fighters because it was thought to have little value over conventional ordnance. The main problem was the lack of suitable Japanese shipping targets to justify its use, although some PBJ-1Js were adapted to take two 'Tiny Tims' below the fuselage. The majority were issued to VMB-612 while it was based on Iwo Jima.

In May 1945 VMB-612 received new PBJ-1Js, and work began

immediately to tailor them – plus some of the older D-models – to the 'Tiny Tim' mission. Modifications included the installation of APG-15 gunsighting equipment for operational testing purposes. In order to check the results obtained with the big rockets several cameras were also fitted into the aircrsft to give the best possible coverage – the PBJ-1J's vacant waist gun positions were utilised for K-19 cameras, as was a ventral hatch aft of the bomb-bay. During May and June some 14 squadron aircraft were converted for 'Tiny Tim' firing.

The rocket launcher system had been developed by the Navy at Inyokern, California, and although it was passed for service with few technical

The 'Tiny Tim' unguided rocket was a new weapon used in action by the PBJs of VMB-612 in the final weeks of the war in the Pacific. North American Aviation thoroughly tested the massive weapon at US Naval Test Center Inkoyern, in California, using a PBH-1H equipped with a lanyard to swing the rocket clear of the aircraft before ignition, prior to clearing it for frontline use (*North American Aviation*)

problems, a PBJ loaded with two of the 11.75-in rockets experienced a ten-knot drag penalty. This meant that flight search sectors had to be slightly shortened.

VMB-612 duly pioneered attack methods and equipment associated with 'Tiny Tim', the unit taking on an important test role. Remaining on Iwo Jima, it awaited orders to relocate forward to Okinawa – a move which placed it nearer to the home islands, and reduced the range to the combat zone.

Potential targets continued to be reported by a variety of sources, and the PBJs undertook 74 low altitude rocket sorties and made 23 anti-shipping attacks in June. There were no losses from combat or on operational training flights.

PBJ crews often left their target areas without knowing how much damage they had inflicted on an enemy vessel. In such cases, though, they could call in help. This happened on 5 June when a Marine Mitchell failed to locate a vessel attacked the previous day until after sunrise. An attack run was initiated but broken off due to the intense flak encountered at the APQ-5 equipment's optimum altitude. The crew radioed a report to base, explaining the flak problem, and VII Fighter Command quickly 'despatched the cavalry' in the form of several P-51s and a PB4Y-2, which attacked the vessel and caused further damage.

By 11 June Lt Col Cram felt confident enough to fly the first test mission with the 'Tiny Tim'. He reported that the PBJ handled well enough with its extra load, but confirmed the ten-knot drag penalty. Throughout the rest of June the squadron continued combat operations, numerous searches resulting in detection of the increasingly smaller vessels the Japanese had been reduced to using to run supplies along the coast from point to point. These were attacked as they were found, often singly or in pairs, but on the 16th the PBJs detected six to eight ships in convoy – a corpeate ccpnteoller the enemy had rarely followed to date. The last vessel was attacked and crippled. The weather denied the PBJ crew a positive sinking report, although radar countermeasures gear indicated not only that their aircraft was under surveillance from shore-based radar on Honshu, but also that the ships in the convoy might have detected them.

The PBJs were now skirting the Tokyo Bay area, where they continued to find small, 175-ft 'Sugar

Special ground-handling teams were assigned to Iwo Jima to prepare the 'Tiny Tims' for loading on to VMB-612's PBJs in mid-1945 (*National Archives*)

After uncrating, the rocket's motor section (light colour) was attached to the warhead (darker colour) using a spanner wrench (*National Archives*)

A modified truck hoist is used to swing the rocket onto its special wheeled trailer (*National Archives*)

A bomb trailer equipped with two screw jacks was used to position the 'Tiny Tims' under the PBJ's belly, this device allowing the rockets to be raised up to the height of the aircraft's weapon shackles. Two of VMB-612's newly-delivered PBJ-1Js, 'White 6' and '5', can been seen in the background of this photograph (*National Archives*)

The rockets were given a thorough checking over prior to their attachment to the aircraft. Here, Sgt Chester T Hunkapiller, VMB-612's NCO in charge of rocket mechanics, operates the front jack on a Mk 51 bomb trailer modified by the squadron to handle the 'Tiny Tims'. 1Lt Richard C Johnson, squadron rocket officer, operates the rear jack (*via Alan Carey*)

Charlie Sugar' and 300-ft 'Fox Tare Dog' and 'Fox Tare Baker' type vessels. They were attacked whenever possible. Larger game presented itself from time to time, and on 26 June a PBJ came upon what was described in reports as a 350-ft destroyer. Two rocket salvoes caused an explosion amidships from the three hits that were observed.

JULY 1945

Life for VMB-612 crews continued much as before, with several positive sightings of Japanese ships, and resulting attacks. With the US fleet operating off Honshu, a joint zone had been established which affected the PBJs' patrol area. The squadron temporarily operated west of the new zone, along the southern coast of Kyushu.

There was further evidence that the enemy had finally adopted a mutually-protective convoy system, but anti-aircraft defence was not always effective. One such sortie on 16 July saw a PBJ attacking one of three destroyer escorts covering a similar number of merchant vessels. Despite the presence of warships, the Marine crew reported no return flak. At the other end of the shipping scale, the PBJs began to note an increasing number of fishing boats near the enemy coast, the smallest usually being left alone. Larger vessels of fishing boat configuration were attacked on the grounds that that they were running war supplies rather than gathering food. By June the squadron's supply of 'Tiny Tims' had been shipped to Okinawa, and no further test flights were made from Iwo Jima.

Cram had meanwhile established his HQ at Chimu Field, on Okinawa, and LSTs and aircraft gradually moved squadron personnel to the new base. Cram himself flew the first VMB-611 mission from Okinawa on 22 July, a search which took the aircraft over the China Sea to the northern tip of Korea. Only a few small fishing boats were seen. On 28 July the squadron's run of zero casualties came to an end with the loss of PBJ-1J BuNo 35242. Carrying a crew of three officers and four

Having been secured to the belly of a PBJ-1D, the 'Tiny Tims' receive their final adjustments prior to the crew starting up and taxiing out. The white fairing above the rockets was probably associated with radar or radio equipment (*via Alan Carey*)

enlisted men, the aircraft was last heard from via VHF radio contact when it was near Hachijo Jima. It had evidently experienced some difficulties (not apparently as a result of enemy action) and was returning to Iwo on one engine. It never arrived.

Missions resumed while the squadron was transferring from one base to another and between 25 and 28 July one 'Fox Tare Charlie' (a 75-ft fishing boat), a sub-chaser and a 125-ft ocean-going tug were attacked. The latter vessel was believed sunk by the aircraft, which then sighted the sub-chaser. Having no rockets left, the PBJ crew went in for a bombing run and dropped a Mk 46 photo flash. A bomb exploded a few feet aft of the vessel's superstructure and undoubtedly caused some crew casualties. Meagre and inaccurate flak from both vessels was reported. A second PBJ also attacked and probably sank a 100-ft Japanese patrol craft.

AUGUST 1945

Time was running short for Japan's war effort. There was also little left for VMB-612 to prove the worth of the 'Tiny Tim' rocket in combat. The unit was hampered by a lack of facilities caused by the moves from Saipan and Iwo Jima, with some equipment, inevitably, having gone missing or been left behind. In any case, operating delicate and temperamental equipment under hostile climatic conditions meant thorough inspections and overhauls – work hampered by inadequate weather protection.

Poor conditions contributed to the damage suffered by a PBJ-1J returning from a sortie on 1 August, the pilot being forced to land in low visibility, with gusty cross-winds on a runway slick with mud. The aircraft bounced heavily on touch down, and when it came into contact with the ground a second time the nose wheel collapsed. No personnel were injured, but the damage extended to a smashed bombardier's compartment and nose wheel door and two bent propellers.

Two PBJs patrolling Tsushima Straits saw only fishing boats on 2 August, and these were not attacked. Aircraft were then grounded due to adverse weather. The first attack of the month was on 5 August, one enemy vessel being damaged. The radar of a second PBJ failed on this mission and a visual search yielded nothing. Further small-scale attacks were made in subsequent days, although the crews had nothing spectacular to report. Two more aircraft on patrol on 10 August reported equipment failure and were forced to return. The following day saw a single PBJ attacking a 'Sugar Baker Sugar' off the western coast of Honshu, near northern Hiroshima. The aircraft fired eight five-inch rockets and four explosions were seen on the vessel.

'TINY TIM'S' DEBUT

On the night of 11/12 August Lt Col Jack Cram carried out VMB-612's first 'Tiny Tim' mission. It turned out to be less than satisfactory, for no vessels large enough even to create a decent radar return were found. However, unwilling to postpone the big rocket's debut any longer, Cram loosed one off at a suitable rock! Whether or not that actually counted went unrecorded in the unit's war diary. Cram repeated this action the following day, another harmless rock succumbing to a 'Tiny Tim' explosion. But Capt Theodore 'Ted' Boutwell was determined to get something with his rockets.

Another VMB-612 PBJ-1J with 'Tiny Tim' rockets in place. Like most Mitchells assigned to the unit, this aircraft has had its dorsal turret and all other guns, except one in the tail, removed (*National Archives*)

He took off on 13 August and headed for the Tsushima Straits. A radar search confirmed the presence of ships, and Boutwell fired off his wing rockets, claiming to have hit two vessels. Still carrying a pair of 'Tims'. he ordered navigator-bombardier MT/Sgt Robert Reed to re-calibrate his sights. A short while later a loud explosion rocked the PBJ, and a check confirmed that the rockets had misfired and exploded, peppering the underside with shrapnel. Under the circumstances, the crew were lucky to have escaped unharmed, and Boutwell had no choice but to return to Okinawa a chastened man, foiled in his quest for a spectacular sinking with a 'Tiny Tim'.

Ideal targets continued to prove elusive, but on the 14th a 200-ft vessel finally presented itself to a PBJ, which attacked immediately. One round was sufficient, the crew witnessing a terrific explosion that was big enough to sink the craft. In this same action a second PBJ went after a group of three ships (all identified as 'Fox Uncles'), two 150-ft in length and one of 250 ft, running parallel with the 200-ft vessel that attacked initially. One hit on each vessel with five-inch rockets was reported, the 'Tiny Tims' apparently firing prematurely. A third aircraft attacked a 'Fox Tare Charlie' with its 'Tims', both of which missed. A repeat run with five-inch rockets resulted in three hits from five rockets, which set the vessel on fire.

On the night of 15-16 August six PBJs ventured into the Tsuchino Straits and attacked a 250-ft 'Fox Tare Charlie'. The results showed that aiming the 'Tims' for effective hits was not so easy, as both rockets carried by the first crew to attack missed. A 'Sugar Charlie Sugar' was also spared the awesome detonation of two more 'Tims'. A third PBJ crew salvoed all eight HVAR wing rockets at a 200-ft vessel of undetermined type, but were unable to observe the results. Finally, a fourth PBJ attacked an unidentified 150-ft vessel with six rockets and scored one hit. This aircraft then made a run on a 350-ft ship, again of undetermined type, and obtained one hit with a 'Tim', which caused extensive damage. And at that point the war finally ended with the Japanese surrender. Officers served beer to the enlisted men in time-honoured tradition, and VMB-612 was released from duty for four-and-a-half days.

WINDING DOWN

The unit maintained a flying rota to keep its collective hand in, and Marine personnel were transported to and from various bases in Japan, including Yokosuka, Honshu, Omura and Kyushu. 'Tiny Tim' test hops were made on 24 and 26 August, Col Cram flying a further six on the 27th. Rockets were now fired over ranges, data being compiled as to release points, missile behaviour and aircraft altitudes. Photographs were taken to record the results obtained.

Lt Col Lawrence F Fox took over as CO of VMB-612 when Jack Cram was transferred to the HQ squadron of MAW-31, effective 1 September.

Aircraft were maintained for a few more weeks, and by the end of October VMB-612 still had an inventory of 18 – five PBJ-1Ds and 13 J-models. But by November flying activity was perceptibly tailing off. The most notable event happened on the 2nd when the squadron executive officer flew to the Chinese coast to obtain weather data. When he returned, a second PBJ was despatched as a navigational escort for 1st Marine Air Wing fighters bound for duty at Tsingtao, again in China. A few days later the squadron received orders terminating its overseas duty.

On the 6th the PBJs were ferried out, the J-models going to a Navy pool (CASU-12) on Guam and the PBJ-1Ds to Awase airfield, Okinawa.

With hostilities at an end, VMB-612's PBJs on Iwo Jima were given a more visible identity in the form of the BuNo number, aircraft designation and branch of service on the outside of both vertical surfaces. This unarmed J-model, complete with 'Tiny Tim' racks, basks in the late summer Pacific sun, its job completed (*National Archives*)

Final steps towards decommissioning were then taken, and at the end of November VMB-612's monthly summary included a simple entry under number of aircraft – 'none'.

MISSION REFLECTIONS

T/Sgt Douglas J Mathieson had shared 1st RRG (radio/radar/gunner) duties on many of Jack Cram's PBJ missions. He added a star in his log book after the unit's first mission, a rocket strike on 13 November 1944. Even in 1988, Mathieson still savoured the elation of that event, as he then recalled to thr author;

'I remember how gung-ho and excited the entire squadron was after hearing about our successful first mission. Flight crews couldn't wait to "get up and at 'em". But I also remember how this attitude soon cooled when all too many of our aircraft failed to return. The grim reality of the business of war was realised forcefully, but we continued to do our job, and do it well.'

Searching out suitable (mainly shipping) targets for rocket attack took VMB-612 to such choice locations as Chichi Jima, Marius Island, Muko Jima and the Inland Sea. Mathieson noted that on two occasions the crew concerned was lucky to 'just make it back' after engine trouble and attention by three Japanese nightfighters. The latter were encountered during a rocket strike mission on 10 February 1945, the PBJ having sighted three enemy destroyers which the fighters may have been escorting. In any event, when Mathieson called out their position using the time-honoured 'clock code', aided by moonlight and visible engine exhaust flames, Cram managed to evade and get the PBJ home safely.

In March 1945 Douglas Mathieson joined a new crew skippered by Lt Baker, for whom he agian served as 1st RRG, with Sgt Meacham as 2nd RRG, T/ Sgt Lee as navigator/bombardier and Cpl Duke as tail gunner. Baker was the pilot on most of the remaining missions, although he appeared to have no personal preference for aircraft, flying several different PBJs on an 'as available' basis. These night sorties included anti-submarine sweeps which took Baker's crew as far as Tokyo Bay, where Japanese shipping under repair was clearly visible. Heavy flak was noted by Mathieson on 9 June, when Baker's PBJ-1D (BuNo 35155) sought out shipping three miles off the Japanese coast. One medium-sized freighter was claimed as hit after four rockets were fired at it.

Although the war was over, VMB-612 continued to test fire the 'Tiny Tim'. However, this PBJ-1J, coded 'White 3', has wing rocket armament, which means that it was probably not one of the squadron's 'Tiny Tim' carriers

On 4 August Mathieson recorded his last PBJ strike mission, a ten-hour flight that took PBJ-1J BuNo 35158 into the Sea of Japan to score two hits on a 300-ft freighter. Mathieson finished his log with another 1988 postscript to this last mission;

'I can remember asking myself what Mrs Mathieson's only son Douglas was doing flying around the Japan Sea, 65 miles south of Vladivostok, Russia!'

VMB-613 IN THE MARSALLS

By January 1945 VMB-613 had arrived at Kwajalein in the Marshall Islands, its 15 PBJ-1Hs led by acting CO Maj George W Nevils. The squadron had spent a similar period in training to the other PBJ units, having been commissioned in October 1943 and subordinated to 9th MAW. Once in the Pacific forward area, VMB-613 became part of 4th MAW, the force at the disposal of the Commander Kwajalein Air Group.

The squadron was far from alone, as the wing had more than a dozen Marine units in the area at that time. This was not an excessive force, for the Marshalls chain includes 100 islands and atolls – only 19 of these were occupied by the Japanese. After the capture of Kwajalein and Eniwetok in February 1944, the US turned its attention away from the Marshalls, leaving airpower to contain those enemy forces left in the islands,

VMB-613 carried out a full-scale strike on Wotje Atoll shortly after its arrival, and then formed 14 PBJs into a squadron detachment that used Eniwetok as a forward base from 31 January 1944. Becoming part of an island sea-air rescue group, the PBJs carried out the first of many routine search operations. The crews were alert for enemy activity in the Kaven Island and Wotje areas, where bypassed Japanese garrisons remained.

Not that these outposts of the Empire posed much of a threat. Most were on their last legs in terms of supplies, with personnel slowly dying of starvation. But they did use the guns for which they still had ammunition when US aircraft passed overhead, and no airman could afford to be complacent. The Carolines had also been largely subdued by army and naval air strikes, and although it had not been necessary to invade this group of small islands and atolls, the remaining Japanese had to be watched and attacked at the slightest sign of hostile activity.

While VMB-613 had a relatively uneventful combat tour, not every mission could be considered a complete 'milk run'. On 6 February a six-aeroplane strike on airfield No 2 (Ponape) resulted in the destruction of PBJ-1H BuNo 35275 flown by Lt William J Love. He was lost with his six-man crew, enemy fire also claiming the navigator of a second participating aircraft. These were the squadron's only combat losses. Worthwhile targets generally remained scarce for the big-gun PBJs, and crews continued to report seeing little of interest during patrols. The Eniwetok detachment ended on 13 March, and all VMB-613 personnel and aircraft returned to Kwajelein.

On the 31st the squadron was detached from MAG-31 and attached to MAG-94 the following day. Forty-eight hours later shipping patrols between Kwajalein and Eniwetok began. Some of these were conducted at maximum range for the PBJs, and therefore carried an element of danger in the event of technical malfunction. Ranging as far as the Bonin Islands (an area that was identified by the codename Dunker's Derby),

VMB-613's PBJ-1Hs formed hunter-killer teams and flew daylight anti-shipping searches. There was still little enemy activity to record, and few technical difficulties appear to have been reported, which was further credit to the Marine groundcrews.

Between 19-28 May four PBJ-1Hs and eight flight crews were ordered to Iwo Jima for a period of daylight anti-shipping patrols with VMB-612. Led by the CO, the detachment's purpose was to determine the feasibility of linking target detection via radar to the 75 mm cannon. Presumably, this was an early form of radar gun-laying, but it appears that technical malfunction, including engine and radio compass problems, prevented any conclusions being reached.

On 1 June the picture changed again for VMB-613 when the squadron began flying night harassment sorties to Mille Atoll. This set the pattern until the end of hostilities, the unit remaining under the command of Lt Col Nevils for the duration of the war.

Despite the unconditional surrender of all Japanese forces, the Allies could not be sure that all outposts of the defeated empire had indeed received the news. On 1 September 1945 two PBJ-1Hs dropped notes to inform the remaining defenders of Wotje and Maloelap Atolls that the war was over. Routine flights continued until 31 October 1945, by which date all PBJ-1Hs had been transferred to CASU-20 at Roi for disposal. VMB-613 was decommissioned on 21 November.

While VMB-613 had been scouring the Marshalls for suitable targets for its cannon, VMB-612 was extending the war to the Japanese home islands. Apart from contact with the enemy, such sorties held other unexpected hazards.

FINALE

Ambitious plans for the patrol bomber element of the Marine Corps were afoot as the war ended. Each air wing would have had its strength boosted to four squadrons of PBJs, two groups of fighters and one of dive-bombers. Each division would have been assigned a separate air wing But this plan anticipated continued enemy resistance, culminating in the invasion of Japan and the war lasting into 1946. When the enemy all but collapsed, and tactical airpower from carriers became so strong, the Marines were obliged to accept a scaling-down of their offensive capability. Garrison duty extended the life of the original PBJ unit slightly beyond the Japanese surrender date, VMB-413 being stationed at Malabang, on Mindanao in the Philippines, during September 1945. The unit was decommissioned at San Diego in November. VMB-423, -433 and -443 also ended up at Malabang during August. All units returned to the US on 30 November and were decommissioned that day.

Although it never saw combat, VMB-614 spent its war on training and weapons testing, which might well have led to deployment had the conflict lasted. The eighth PBJ squadron to be commissioned (on 10 October 1943), its duties included extensive torpedo testing using old, war-weary PBJs handed on by the MOTS (Marine Operational Training Squadrons) at NAS Boca Chica and Cherry Point. Night radar bombing practice was also conducted at Houma, Louisiana.

Overseas movement orders came in mid-1945, and from Ewa VMB-614 moved across the central Pacific to Midway, where the air and ground echelons were reunited on 31 August. VMB-614 had moved around awaiting the call to arms that never came. This situation led to the adoption of the nickname 'Sixty-Million Dollar Squadron', because that was how much the personnel reckoned the government had spent on their training!

The Corps commissioned a total of 16 PBJ units during the war – four more in the '600 series' range and a further four in the '400 series'. These were, respectively, VMB-621, -622, -623 and -624, and -453, -463, -473 and -483. All were commissioned at Cherry Point to undertake a training role. As far as the MOTS were concerned, VMB-811, -812, -813 and -814 were commissioned specifically to train SNB and PBJ crews after the first combat units had been established in 1943. All '800 series' PBJ units were commissioned at Edenton on 1 January 1944, but they had originally started life as VMB-621, -622, -623 and -624, respectively.

CARRIER BORNE?

Had the invasion of Japan happened, PBJs might have been equipped for launching from carriers for strikes on the home islands. Ever since Doolittle's Tokyo Raid of April 1942, the Navy had maintained a link with the B-25, which for some time remained the largest and heaviest aircraft to have made a deck take-off. This one-off mission had provided useful data, but the relative ease of launching from a carrier – numerous single-engined aircraft without a tail hook had made such one way trips during the war – became more complex if landing back on board was required.

To test the feasibility of a heavy twin doing so, PBJ-1H 43-4700 (BuNo 35277) was fitted with a hook for trials with the USS *Shangri-La* (CV-38) in November 1944. North American Aviation's Kansas City modification centre undertook the necessary structural strengthening, and the Naval Air Materiel Center (NAMC) at Philadelphia installed the equipment.

Lt Cdr H S Bottomley lands a PBJ-1H on the deck of the USS *Shangri-La* (CV-38) in November 1944 as part of a programme which anticipated the launch of medium bombers from carriers had the war continued into 1946 (*North American Aviation*)

The PBJ is just moments away from being successfully 'hooked' by one of *Shangri-La's* deck wires after landing-on. The bomber was fitted with special main wheel axles which allowed a greater than normal degree of manoeuvring on the carrier deck
(*North American Aviation*)

Sea trials with the PBJ, a P-51D and the Grumman F7F-1 were conducted by NAMC on 15 November 1944. Lt Cdr H S Bottomley landed the PBJ aboard after a few anxious moments that had seen the first approach aborted and the aircraft returned to NAS Norfolk for repair.

On the second attempt Bottomley engaged the wire and the aircraft ran 120 ft down the deck before coming to a halt. The Navy and North American Aviation made a close inspection of the PBJ, which had been specially fitted with wheels that could turn sideways to a limited degree to ease taxiing on deck. For re-launch, the PBJ weighed 27,000 lb. A second landing aimed for an off-centre touch down, which Bottomley achieved, although not without some damage – this included the loss of a main wheel door on the last take-off. After a successful third launch, the PBJ's 'sea trials' came to an end. Although it too was destined for a shore-based role in Marine Corps service, the F7F Tigercat weighed in at 25,720 lbs gross compared with 34,000 lbs for a fully loaded PBJ-1.

The carrier-borne PBJ experiment ended on what some considered to be a rather disappointing note when it was decided that Marine air would henceforth be restricted primarily to short range, close support. That meant no requirement for multi-engined bombers. The F7F met the need for a longer-range fighter, but bombers were considered a significant step further. They were costly to procure, man and maintain in the austere post-war period. But if a case had to be made for longer ranging bombers being operated by the Corps, which because of its amphibious operations required both short and long range air support, then the PBJ had surely proven its worth, particularly in the fight for the Philippines.

But it was a fact of life that jet propulsion was making frontline piston-engine aircraft all but obsolete. North American's reliable old medium bomber was far from unique in being overtaken by progress.

By the end of 1945 six of the seven operational PBJ units had been disbanded and the remaining personnel transferred to other units. With the decommissioning of VMB-612 on 14 March 1946, the PBJ Mitchell became little more than a memory in the history of Marine Corps aviation.

The end is nigh. PBJ-1D trainers line up awaiting their fate after the war, probably at NAS Clinton, in Oklahoma. All are in natural aluminium finish, with black ID numbers on the nose and tail
(*National Archives*)

That may have been the case when the squadrons were disbanded. But the B-25/PBJ was so widely used that a substantial number survived the mass scrapping process after the war and some PBJs were used for munitions testing.

Indeed, the Navy used the PBJ-1H for 'Tiny Tim' tests, and at least one J-model was modified to carry out a series of test shoots with a 'rocket gun' built into the aircraft's nose. Aligned on the PBJ's centreline, the device comprised an automatic launcher for five-inch spin-stabilised rockets that could be salvoed (five or six rounds) at 0.3 second intervals from a rotating drum magazine. The tests at China Lake did not convince observers that it was effective enough to enter production.

Finale. **Hundreds of PBJs line up for disposal at NAS Clinton, their fate being marginally more dignified than that which befell VMB-611's war-weary machines at Ford Island, Hawaii – the latter were simply shoved off the dockside into the water, much to the temporary horror of onlooking veteran PBJ crews from the unit** (*National Archives*)

A handful of Marine Mitchells flew on well into the late 1940s, this particular PBJ-1J being involved in a Navy programme to evaluate a built-in 'gun' which fired spin-stabilised rockets. Cameras recorded the firing sequence and the dramatic flash as the missiles left the barrel (*North American Aviation via N Avery*)

APPENDICES

APPENDIX A

PBJ BuNo NUMBERS

PBJ-1C BuNos 34998 to 35047 (50)

PBJ-1D BuNos 35048 to 35072 (25)
PBJ-1D BuNos 35078 to 35096 (24)
PBJ-1D BuNos 35098 to 35193 (96)
PBJ-1D BuNos 35196 to 35202 (7)

PBJ-1G BuNo 35097 (1)

PBJ-1H BuNos 35250 to 35297 (48)
PBJ-1H BuNos 88872 to 89071 (200)

PBJ-1J BuNos 35194 and 35195 (2)
PBJ-1J BuNos 35203 to 35249 (47)
PBJ-1J BuNos 35798 to 35920 (123)
PBJ-1J BuNos 38980 to 39012 (33)
PBJ-1J BuNos 64943 to 64992 (50)

Total aircraft allocated – 706 (687 actually delivered)

APPENDIX B

MARKINGS AND IDENTITIES

VMB-413
Markings: individual PBJ-1C/Ds (when based on Stirling Island) used call signs '40-B-22' to '49-B-22', and had last two digits of their BuNo painted (in white or black, i.e. BuNo 35126 had '26' in black) under the cockpit windows, these machines being in standard Navy light blue and white camouflage. Only bomb logs were officially permitted, and most, if not all, crews seemed to have complied with this
Representative aircraft
Original aircraft (PBJ-1D/J): BuNos 35074, 35101, 35123, 35126, 35128, 35129, 35134, 35135, 35143, 35146, 35151, 35160, 35163, 35166, 35169, 35187, 35190, 35191, 35192, 35199 and 35233

VMB-423
Markings: PBJ-1D in standard patrol bomber camouflage, two-digit numbers on forward fuselage below cockpit

VMB-433
Markings: PBJ-1D in standard patrol bomber camouflage

VMB-443
Markings: PBJ-1D in standard patrol bomber camouflage

VMB-611
Markings: PBJ-1D in standard early and late patrol bomber camouflage
Representative aircraft
PBJ-1D/J: BuNos 35166, 35178, 35185, 35188, 35191, 35198, 35217, 38983, 38998, 39006 and 64951

VMB-612
Markings: PBJ-1D in standard camouflage and overall sea blue schemes. Squadron was assigned at least 69 PBJs during its career, and at an unknown date the original two-digit radio call numbers ('Mike Baker 26', '29' and so on), which were not based on the BuNo, were replaced by single numbers to improve clarity. Thus, Col Cram's aircraft marked 'MB-26' became 'MB-0'. The 'MB' prefix was dropped when the squadron received PBJ-Js, aircraft then being identified by one- or two-digit numbers painted on each fin at approximately mid point
Representative aircraft
PBJ-1D: BuNo 35150/MB-41 (post-war transfer to MAG-22)
CO Jack Cram regularly flew two PBJ-1Ds, BuNos 35167/MB-0 and MB-26 and BuNo 35156/MB-36. By contrast, Lt Baker flew his missions in at least nine different PBJ-1Js, namely BuNos 35139, 35148, 35170, 35239, 35158, 35154, 35234, 35155 and 35167
PBJ-1J: 35234; 35239; 35242; 35836; 35837

VMB-613
Markings: PBJ-1Hs in standard three-tone scheme as far as is known. Large white two-digit numerals on lower half of fin and rudder (probably based on BuNo number) denoted individual aircraft
Representative aircraft
PBJ-1Hs BuNos 35275 and 88922

VMB-614
No markings details confirmed

APPENDIX C

COMBAT CASUALTIES

A total of 99 PBJ Mitchells were lost to all causes during the Marines' association with the type. The following list of crashes involving crew fatalities is presented primarily to provide an aide memoire to the type and identity of the aircraft involved

Date	Unit	Aircraft identity	Pilot/Remarks
22/1/44	VMB-413	PBJ-1C BuNo 35131/31	Lt S M Duval/non-combat cause
8/2/44	VMB-443	PBJ-1D BuNo 35088	1Lts Clifford McClinton and Frank Crummer Jr
3/3/44	VMB-423	PBJ-1D BuNo 35154	1Lt Henry E Seeman
22/3/44	VMB-413	PBJ-1C BuNo 35124/24	Maj J K Smith
22/3/44	VMB-413	PBJ-1C BuNo 35117/17	Lt William Gaul
2/4/44	VMB-413	PBJ-1D BuNo 35134	Capt Rex A Dresher
20/4/44	VMB-423	PBJ-1D BuNo 35083	1Lt Alden R Carlson
21/4/44	VMB-413	PBJ-1D BuNo 35127	Maj D E Keeler
22/4/44	VMB-423	PBJ-1D BuNo 35087	1Lt Laverne A Lallathin
5/5/44	VMB-413	PBJ-1C BuNo 35143/43	Lt Glenn W Smith/flak at Tobera
22/6/44	VMB-423	PBJ-1D BuNo 35109	1Lt Vernon S Buckley Jr
29/6/44	VMB-423	PBJ-1D BuNo 35141	Capt Richard A Edmonds
29/7/44	VMB-413	PBJ-1C (BuNo unknown)	Bob Millington/flak Choiseul
6/8/44	VMB-433	PBJ-1D BuNo 35114	1Lt C W Sieben/MAG-61 crew
2/9/44	VMB-433	PBJ-1D BuNo 35106	1Lts Charles L Ingels and Richard R Graves
11/9/44	VMB-443	PBJ-1D BuNo 35100	1Lt Eric E Terry Jr
17/9/44	VMB-443	PBJ-1 (BuNo unknown)	1Lts Benjamin G Kinnick and Dominic F Bellanca
16/11/44	VMB-612	PBJ-1D BuNo 35201	2Lt James W Bostick
27/11/44	VMB-612	PBJ-1D BuNo 35156	1Lts Edward Madray and James W Robbins
29/11/44	VMB-612	PBJ-1D BuNo 35149	1Lts Cleo J Falgout and John R Johnston
29/11/44	VMB-612	PBJ-1 (BuNo unknown)	Lt Edward Madray
17/1/45	VMB-611	PBJ-1D BuNo 35175/MB-5	Lt Charles H Lawrence/crew KIA
6/2/45	VMB-613	PBJ-1H BuNo 35275	1Lts William J Love and Thomas W Stone
11-12/2/45	VMB-612	PBJ-1D BuNo 35168	Lt Clifford James/crew KIA in night mission
27/2/45	VMB-413	PBJ-1D (BuNo unknown)	Lt George P Boyes
27/2/45	VMB-433	PBJ-1D BuNo 35105	1Lt Donald R Harpley
16/4/45	VMB-612	PBJ-1D BuNo 35161	2Lt Elwood D Peters and S/Sgt Clinton E Crain/downed by F4U Corsairs
21/4/45	VMB-413	PBJ-1 (BuNo unknown)	Maj D E Keeler/non-combat cause
22/4/45	VMB-612	PBJ-1D (BuNo unknown)	Lts Samuel Balthrop and Joseph J Bottalico/crew KIA
2/5/45	VMB-611	PBJ-1 (BuNo unknown)	1Lts Robert B Mason and Paul A Frank
2/5/45	VMB-612	PBJ-1 BuNo 35196	1Lt John Jarrell
5/5/45	VMB-413	PBJ-1 (BuNo unknown)	Maj G W Smith
30/5/45	VMB-611	PBJ-1D BuNo 35164/MB-11	Lt Col George A Sarles/CO and three crew KIA
19/6/45	VMB-611	PBJ-1D BuNo 35172	1Lt Robert A Griffith
27/7/45	VMB-612	PBJ-1 (BuNo unknown)	Lts Myron C Peterson and Calvin A Swallow

Note
Some of the above ranks may be at variance with official records and personal recollections

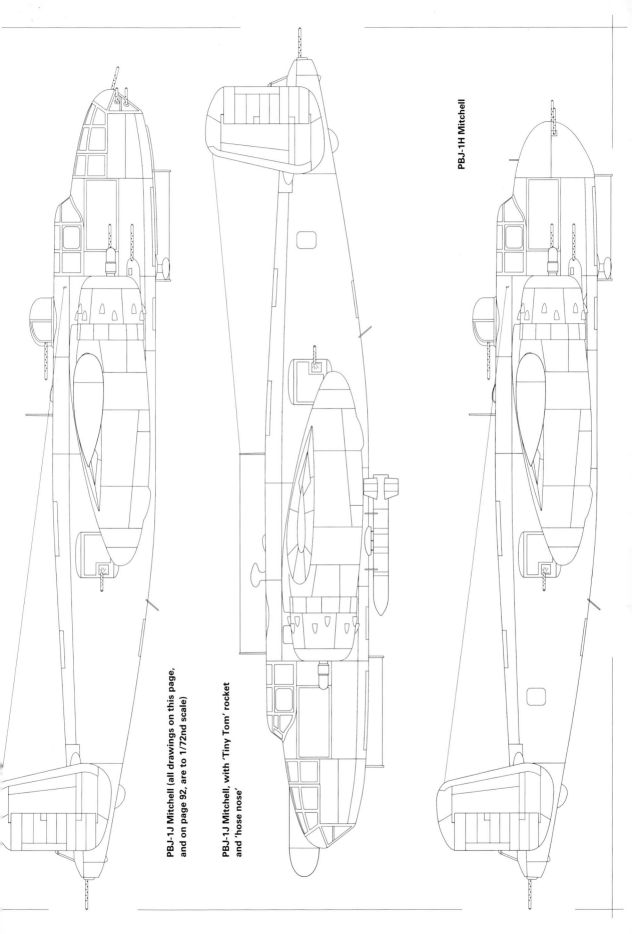

PBJ-1J Mitchell (all drawings on this page, and on page 92, are to 1/72nd scale)

PBJ-1J Mitchell, with 'Tiny Tom' rocket and 'hose nose'

PBJ-1H Mitchell

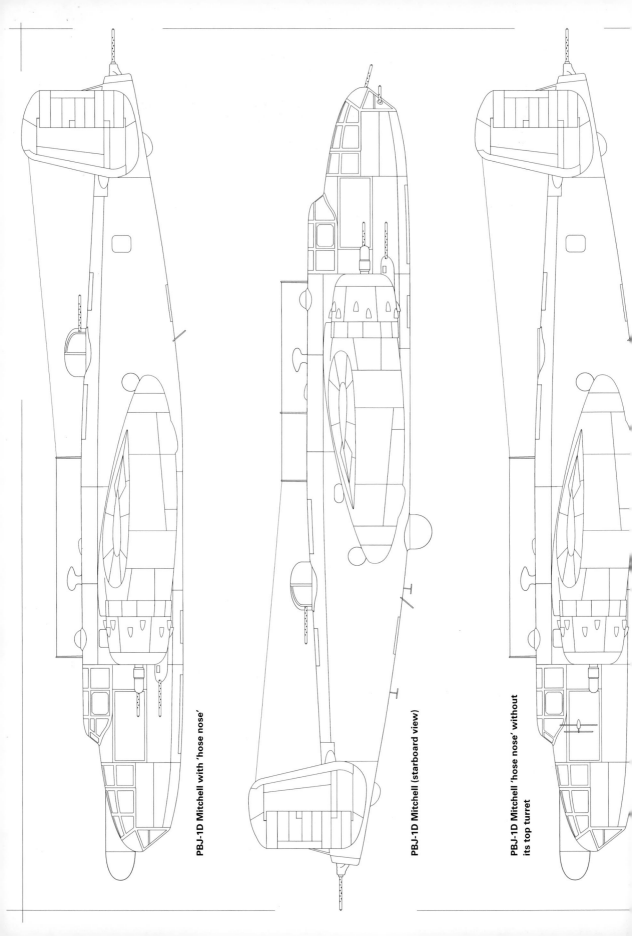

PBJ-1D Mitchell with 'hose nose'

PBJ-1D Mitchell (starboard view)

PBJ-1D Mitchell 'hose nose' without its top turret

Author's Note

It is still difficult to tie in PBJ markings, such as they were, with BuNo numbers, and the anonymity of many of the aircraft depicted in profile in this volume confirms that we still have some way to go in this aspect of Marine air operations in World War 2. Indeed, PBJs remain largely anonymous in this important respect – small wonder when bureau numbers were applied in digits only four inches high, thus making them all but impossible to read even in good quality photographs!

1

PBJ-1C of Operational Training Squadron 8, MCAS Cherry Point, North Carolina, 1943

This PBJ-1C is representative of the aircraft that made up the first batch of 50 B-25C equivalents delivered as part of Navy contracts and passed to the Marine Corps mainly for training. It is a virtually standard USAAF aircraft apart from the US Navy patrol bomber camouflage of medium blue-grey topsides and light grey undersides. Note that the retractable ventral gun turret has been displaced by a radar scanner.

2

PBJ-1D BuNo 35094 *JONAH,* MCAS Cherry Point, North Carolina, 1944

This PBJ-1D, named *JONAH*, was fitted with a retractable ventral scanner for APS-3 sea search radar and flew numerous tests with a standard naval torpedo slung under the bomb-bay. The doors partially closed on the weapon, which was dropped via a mechanism installed in the bay itself and aimed via a special sight in the cockpit. In the event, no PBJ ever dropped a torpedo in anger.

3

PBJ-1C 'White 61' of Operational Training Squadron 8, MCAS Cherry Point, North Carolina, 1943

This PBJ-1C displays a hastily-daubed aircraft number for flightline recognition. The Marines had to create a medium bomber programme at short notice, and neat and tidy aircraft markings had low priority. '61' was probably the last two digits of the aircraft's Bureau of Aeronautics serial number.

4

PBJ-1D 'White 11' of an unidentified Operational Training Squadron, MCAS Cherry Point, North Carolina, 1944

Seen on the Cherry Point flightline in 1944, this aircraft also has standard Navy/USMC patrol bomber finish, with the previously red national insignia outline retouched with insignia blue. The PBJ-1D introduced wing racks for bombs or depth charges, adding a 1000-lb ordnance 'punch' to the internal load.

5

PBJ-1D 'White R109' of an unidentified Operational Training Squadron, MCAS Edenton, North Carolina, 1944

Painted up in a typical PBJ training scheme, this aircraft's prominent 'R109' code served the dual purpose of aiding air-to-air recognition and discouraging unauthorised low flying. Like many PBJs, it retains the gun gas dispersion tube below the nose, despite the overpainted clear panels.

6

PBJ-1D 'White K108' of an unidentified Operational Training Squadron, MCAS Edenton, North Carolina, 1944

This machine is marked similarly to the 'R' prefixed aircraft seen in the previous profile. As the PBJ programme settled into a routine, aircraft markings became standardised and training units used letters and numbers to identify bases or training squadrons, as shown here. The national insignia has the red outline, used between June and August 1943, overpainted with fresh insignia blue, hence the darker outline on an obviously more faded blue background.

7

PBJ-1D 'Black 310' of VMB-433, South-West Pacific, 1944

This was one among many Marine Mitchells in Marine Air Group 61 where the crew recorded their missions as small bomb silhouettes adjacent to the pilot's cockpit. This time-honoured bomb log was very rarely backed by any further personalisation, although the decorated propeller hub(s) (in red, white and blue) represent a modest identification marking duplicated on several squadron aircraft.

8

PBJ-1D 'Black 03' of VMB-423, Green Island, South-West Pacific, 1944

Continuous missions to Rabaul, Kavieng and other bypassed Japanese bastions meant that mission credits for individual aircraft accumulated rapidly. An unknown number of Marine Mitchells flew 100 missions or more, this aircraft being just one example.

9

PBJ-1D BuNo 35138 'Black 38' of VMB-423, South-West Pacific, 1944

Tough, reliable and able to withstand a fair amount of combat damage, the PBJ-1D served the Marines well, and although its performance was never earth-shattering, it proved that the Corps could handle missions other than 'traditional' close air support. This aircraft belonged to VMB-423, and had the distinction of being the first PBJ to achieve the 100-mission mark, on 25 November 1944.

10
PBJ-1D 'White MB 6' of VMB-612, MCAS Boca Chica, North Carolina, 1944
The most distinctive marking applied to PBJs was arguably the 'MB' prefix applied to aircraft flown by both VMB-611 and -612. The letters, which probably stemmed from the simple 'Marine Bomber' or 'Mike Baker' abbreviation, were referred to in the frontline even when they were not painted on! This PBJ-1D of VMB-612 had its codes applied in the US, and these were abbreviated to just the numerals when the unit went overseas. By contrast, VMB-611 generally retained the letters in-theatre.

11
PBJ-1D 'White MB 11' of VMB-611, Mindanao, the Philippines, 1944-45
A darker panel behind the nose code on this PBJ-1D ('Mike Baker 11' of VMB-611) may have been a deliberate move to make the code stand out for the benefit of the groundcrews during pre-mission preparation. One clear indicator that the early PBJ nose coding was not sufficient for air-to-air recognition was the repeat application of the aircraft number on the fin.

12
PBJ-1J *LASSIE* of VMB-433, South-West Pacific, 1944
A rare example of nose art on VMB-433's PBJ-1J, *LASSIE* proved the exception to a widely adhered-to rule for Marine crews not to deface government property. This may not have been strictly enforced, but artwork and names on PBJs in combat areas were rare.

13
PBJ-1J *RAGGEDY ANN* (training unit unknown), flown by Al Sullivan, Hawaii, 1944
This is a further example of nose art on a PBJ-1J, the aircraft operating with an unidentified training unit from a base in Hawaii in 1944, where it was flown by an instructor by the name of Al Sullivan. It seems that artwork was tolerated in rear areas and in training squadrons to a greater extent than in the frontline. Even so, there is little photographic evidence that Marine flyers ever indulged in a rash of garish or risqué names and artwork, as was common in the USAAF.

14
PBJ-1J 'Black 220' of VMB-611, Mindanao, the Philippines, 1945
The eight-gun strafer nose designed to fit all B-25/PBJ models was rarely seen in wartime photographs of Marine Mitchells, and of the handful of examples captured on film, most of these were PBJ-1J models. Factory-supplied kits could be fitted as field modifications, as is believed to have been the case with this particular example. Nicknamed 'Sarles' Raiders' after its popular CO, VMB-611 flew numerous strafing sorties in the Philippines.

15
PBJ-1H of US Naval Test Center Inyokern, California, 1945-46
Although they tried their best, Marine commanders could find little practical employment for the PBJ-1H, which had its armament built around a powerful 75 mm cannon. The big gun ideally required more worthwhile targets than the crews of VMB-613 – the only unit operational with the H-model – could find. It was in the testing of 'Tiny Tim' rockets and performing other trials that the PBJ-1H proved most useful, and this example was employed in post-war rocket testing at Inyokern.

16
PBJ-1H 'White 99' of VMB-614, MCAS Ewa, Hawaii mid-1945
When it was declared operational, VMB-614 adopted a different identification system to other PBJ units, the squadron adorning its aircraft with large white tail numbers as shown here. It also appears to have been the rule that the H-models it flew were identical to standard USAAF B-25Hs in most respects apart from the installation of radar on the right wingtip. Once in-theatre, VMB-614 undertook a series of flights in order to integrate the PBJs' radar returns with cannon operation, but a lack of shipping targets generally frustrated this effort.

17
PBJ-1H BuNo 35277 of the Naval Air Materiel Center, Philadelphia, 1944
Unique in being the only PBJ-1H to land on a carrier deck, this aircraft put down on the USS *Shangri-La* in November 1944 as part of a series of tests involving both Army and Navy aircraft. Apart from the tail hook, the aircraft had modified main wheel axles to allow greater castoring on deck in anticipation of possible future launchings of fully laden PBJs against Japan.

18
PBJ-H BuNo 35291 (USAAF 43-4482) of North American Aviation, USA, 1944
This PBJ-1H (AAF s/n 43-4482, BuNo 35291) is equipped with radar and finished in sea blue overall, yet it displays its army rather than BuNo serial number. The reason for this apparent contradiction is unknown, although a PBJ-1J also flew in a similar finish, and both aircraft may have been engaged in a North American Aviation flight test programme prior to their delivery to the Marines. This aircraft was only the second PBJ-1H on Navy contracts for the Marines, which may explain its markings anomaly.

19
PBJ-1D 'White 9' of VMB-612, Saipan and Iwo Jima, 1945
If a Mitchell could be modified then the Marines invariably did so, adding features of their own. It should, however, be stressed that North American Aviation and the USAAF had carried out most of the modification work prior to the first PBJ seeing

combat. For example, the fitting of J/H-model waist gun windows was quite commonplace on B-25Ds and PBJ-1Ds, although the 'hose nose' radar configuration remained unique to the Corps.

20
PBJ-1J 'White 10' of VMB-612, Saipan, spring 1945
Not all of VMB-612's PBJs were adapted to carry 'Tiny Tims', nor did they all have their dorsal guns removed – there was less need for gun defence when the squadron moved to Iwo Jima in mid-1945, where the dorsal turret was removed. Still boasting its 'top' turret, this PBJ-1J was the not untypical exception to a general rule for the squadron's aircraft when based on Saipan and Iwo Jima in mid-1945.

21
PBJ-1D 'White 5' of VMB-612, Saipan and Iwo Jima, 1945
A more conformist PBJ-1D, 'White 5' reflects the VMB-612 practice of reducing aircraft identification right down to a single number – in fact numbers were revised over a previous series using two-digit numbers. That said, the numerals stood out well enough on the dark blue background of the fin. Devoid of package or turret guns, this aircraft's main armament was the favoured battery of eight HVARs, plus a single 'fifty' in the extreme tail.

22
PBJ-1D 'White 8' of VMB-612, Saipan and Iwo Jima, 1945
This aircraft displays an unusual, but appropriate, method of recording missions by the application of miniature rocket sihouettes. As with other air forces, the Marines proved the HVAR to be highly effective against a variety of land and sea targets. It had 'stand-off' characteristics that were highly appreciated by crews who did not have to fly straight through flak as they might have done when delivering bombs. Data shows that at least one other VMB-612 aircraft recorded its missions in this way.

23
PBJ-1J BuNo 64973 'White 0' of VMB-612, Iwo Jima, 1945
When the war ended, higher authority was quick to direct the PBJ squadrons to make the aircraft designation, BuNo number and the branch of service indication more visible. Although this move may have seemed a little superfluous in the middle of the Pacific, it did mark a return to peace, and the right of civilians to identify and report military aircraft for unauthorised low flying, or 'buzzing'. This PBJ-1J on Iwo Jima in August 1945 – one of VMB-612's 'Tiny Tim' carriers, complete with a K-19 camera in the waist – conformed to the new markings directive. Repainting took time, and had a low priority when set against the euphoria of victory and a general slackening of pace, although 'Cram's Rams' were not immediately put out to grass on VJ-Day.

24
PBJ-1D 'Black 049' of an unidentified Operational Training Squadron, NAS Clinton, Oklahoma, 1945
Training units in the US persevered with training PBJ crews through to the end of the war because in the spring of 1945 it was uncertain when the conflict would come to an end. Stripping off the camouflage paint gave PBJ-1D radar trainers such as '049' a few extra miles per hour of speed, and as the programme broadened, more easily-read identification numbers were adopted. This aircraft ended up at NAS Clinton in 1945.

Back cover
PBJ-1J BuNo 35849 (USAAF 44-30980) of the US Naval Ordnance Station China Lake, California, 1945-46
A hybrid PBJ-1J that had been stripped of its camouflage, this aircraft was used by the Navy in a post-war rocket launcher test programme. A strafer nose enclosed the barrel of the weapon, which automatically pumped out the rockets from a centreline tube. As with other innovative weapons developed in the final year of the war, this equipment was not adopted in peacetime.

INDEX

References to illustrations are shown in **bold**. Plates are shown with page and caption locators in brackets.